The MAE WEST FILMS

By
JAMES L. NEIBAUR

The Mae West Films
By James L. Neibaur

Published in the USA by:
BearManor Media
1317 Edgewater Dr #110
Orlando, FL 32804
www.bearmanormedia.com

Paperback ISBN: 979-8-88771-393-9
Hardback ISBN: 979-8-88771-394-6
BearManor Media, Orlando, Florida
Printed in the United States of America
Book design by Robbie Adkins, www.adkinsconsult.com
This is a book of scholarship. All photos used in this book are for chapters offering criticism and commentary.

TABLE OF CONTENTS

ACKNOWLEDGEMENTS

First and foremost, I have to thank my wonderful, hardworking assistant Katie Carter. Katie is a film critic, historian, and scholar in her own right who lives each book with me, watching every movie, going over every chapter, offering her own ideas and fixing my (many) typos. These books benefit tremendously from her help. She is quoted throughout this study.

Thanks to my friend Steve Stoliar, who wrote a book about his years as Groucho Marx's secretary that recalls a meeting between Groucho and Mae West in the 1970s. Steve gave me permission to share this incident from his book.

Thanks to my dedicatee Farran Smith Nehme who helped to inspire this book.

Further appreciation goes to Gary Schneeberger, Ted Okuda, Jill Blake, Peter Jackel, Terri Lynch, Allie Schulz, Kelly Parmelee, Kim Morgan, Laura Grieve, Christopher Riordan, Phil Hall, Leonard Maltin, the late Brian Phillips, the late Jerry Lewis, and the memory of my late wife Diana and late son Max, both of whom will forever inspire all that I do.

DEDICATION

To my friend Farran Smith Nehme.

Thanks for constantly expanding my knowledge of film history
with your intelligence and insight

INTRODUCTION

Mae West is a true show business icon, and while her screen career netted comparatively few movies, it is those that we have to assess her legacy. This book will focus on her film career with a chapter on each movie. There will also be an introductory chapter on her long stage career and how it led to her entrance into films, and chapters about her work when not appearing in films, discussing how she continued to cultivate her image and stardom during years-long gaps offscreen.

Mae West performed on the vaudeville stage and later made it to Broadway with plays and revues that she created herself. Becoming famous as a sex symbol, West boldly stepped over the edge. Her first starring role on Broadway was in *Sex,* a highly risqué show that she wrote, directed, and produced as well as starred in. While critics and special interest groups condemned the show, general audiences bought up a lot of tickets, making it a hit. The show was raided and West was arrested on a morals charge. She accurately recognized it as great publicity. Further shows like *Diamond Lil* and *The Constant Sinner* resulted in further negative reactions from religious groups and more conservative circles, while the general public was captivated.

When Mae West entered movies in 1932, she quickly conquered that medium, being allowed to write her own dialog and have some creative control over her character, due to her already significant notoriety. Her films were huge hits, but once the production code began being more powerfully enforced in 1934, her battles with the censors became as notable as the films in which she was appearing. West successfully returned to the stage in the later 1930s, but after a controversial appearance on a popular radio show, she was banned from the airwaves.

Returning to films when summoned by Universal to co-star with W.C. Fields in *My Little Chickadee* (1940), West's battles with

Fields were legendary, and often exaggerated. Despite whatever conflicts, the teaming of these two great stars resulted in a movie that has lived on as a classic example of either.

Mae West's film career did not conclude, but pretty much sputtered, with the lackluster *The Heat's On* (1943), the disastrous *Myra Breckinridge* (1969), and finally her own *Sextette* (1978), a notorious flop. She died in 1980.

As this book explores her screen career film-by-film, the text will also discuss her stage work, appearances on radio and television, and her living long enough to enjoy young college-aged fans in the 1970s discovering her past work.

Mae West is one of the great stars of the 20th century, and fortunately, the relatively few films Mae West appeared in give us a good idea of her talent, her style, and her impact.

MAE WEST BEFORE THE MOVIES

The focus of this text is Mae West's film career, but some information about her early life and her work on stage is still necessary. While there are other books that will examine this period of West's life and career more thoroughly, this book will discuss her stage work where she created and honed her character, and aroused a great deal of controversy with her edgy Broadway shows. Mae West was already a star when she entered movies in 1932.

Mae West was born Mary Jane West on August 17, 1893 in Brooklyn, New York. Her mother, Mathilde, was a fashion model and her father, John (aka Jack), was a prizefighter with his own private investigation business. Mae had an innate talent and a real knack for entertaining at a very young age. She was already performing in local talent shows by the age of 5 as Baby Mae, and by the age of 14 she was working in vaudeville. Mae worked in smaller units, including the Hal Clarendon Stock Company where she got her start, and Gus Sun Booking Exchange, which was active in the Midwest. It was in vaudeville where Mae was allowed to explore a lot of creative ideas while trying to land on one that worked best for her. Influenced by popular female impersonators Bert Savoy and Julian Eltinge, Mae developed her trademark walk while performing in vaudeville shows.

Mae West's first appearance on Broadway was in 1911 when she was 18 years old. Although the show closed after eight performances, *The New York Times* stated that "Mae West, hitherto unknown, pleased by her grotesquerie and snappy way of singing and dancing."[1] This unsuccessful show was successful for her, as it helped advance her vaudeville career.

---

1 Leonard, Maurice. *Mae West Empress of Sex*. NY: Harper Collins, 1991

In 1912, Mae West appeared in a show at the Palace in Bangor, Maine and netted a headline writeup in their local newspaper:

> A brilliant audience sat in the Bijou last night to see Mae West to note her lavishly advertised gowns…. And evidently, they liked what they saw and heard, for the applause was frequent. She is typical of the gay life of Broadway. You see her prototypes in the feverish, scintillating, clever entertainments of the Winter Garden and the Moulin Rouge. In short, Mae West is something more than a professional beauty; she is original and interesting…. Everyone will go to see her this week, and we think they will like her.[2]

In 1913, Mae West appeared in a show at the Proctor's Palace Theater in Newark, New Jersey, which was headlined by ex-boxer James J. "Gentleman Jim" Corbett. The local newspaper lauded her performance:

> Mae West is a complete revelation. She has been hailed by critics as a second Eva Tanguay,[3] but in reality, Eva looks like a poor counterfeit of Mae West. Miss West has a most pleasing personality, is clever in her talk and actions, and when she sings, she wins.[4]

In 1916 she opened in New York with an act called "Mae West and Sister" which played at the Broadway theater Fifth Avenue in Manhattan. The *Variety* critic said at the time:

> Mae West in big time vaudeville may only be admired for her persistency in believing she is a big time act and trying to make vaudeville accept her as such. Unless Miss West can tone down her stage presence in every way, she just might as well hop right out of vaudeville into burlesque. The act did very well at the Fifth Avenue

---

2 Mae West – Very Clever Woman. *The Bangor Daily*. December 17, 1912

3 Canadian born Tanguay was a top vaudeville star at the time, known as The Queen of Vaudeville.

4 Corbett, Mae West, Many More at Proctor's. *Newark Star-Eagle*. September 23, 1913.

Mae West on the cover of sheet music

on Tuesday Afternoon. Mae responded to the applause with a speech. She said: "I am very pleased, ladies and gentlemen, you liked my new act. It's the first time I have appeared with my sister. They all like her, especially the boys who always fall for her. But that's where I come in – I always take them away from her."[5]

5 New Acts This Week. *Variety*. July, 11, 1916

Mae West's career advanced to the Shubert Brothers revue *Sometime* which starred Ed Wynn. Performing a dance for the song "Ev'rybody Shimmies Now," Mae's face was placed on the cover of the sheet music. *The New York Herald,* in their review of this show, stated: "Three of the players stood out as special favorites: Ed Wynn, Francine Larimore and Mae West."

Mae West's stardom shot up greatly during the 1920s when she began writing her own plays under the pen name Jane Mast. Her first starring role on Broadway was in the play *Sex,* which she also wrote. Produced by C. William Morganstern and directed by Edward Elsner, *Sex* was a comedy-drama that dealt with prostitutes, pimps, crooked cops, and other figures, while the narrative was filled with risqué situations. Critics wrote scathing reviews, and religious groups protested, but that only ignited greater interest in the production. Broadway had been in a slump, and *Sex* turned that around. Despite bad press, the play opened in April of 1926 and was the only Broadway show that ran successful through the summer and into the following year. The only reason it closed in March of 1927 is because law enforcement had it stopped after 375 performances and the entire cast, including Mae West, was arrested on moral charges. Mae took a jail sentence (10 days in a workhouse) rather than pay the affordable $500 fine because she realized the publicity could be effective.

Her next play *The Drag* dealt with homosexuality, and after trial runs in Connecticut and New Jersey, plans to bring the show to New York were thwarted by law enforcement. West tried to rework it as *Pleasure Man* but after an October, 1928 premiere in Queens, the entire cast was arrested for indecency.

Diamond Lil became perhaps Mae West's biggest Broadway hit, and she revived it often, even using it as the basis for her film *She Done Him Wrong.* It first opened at the Royale Theater on Broadway in April of 1928 and ran until January of 1929. It was this play

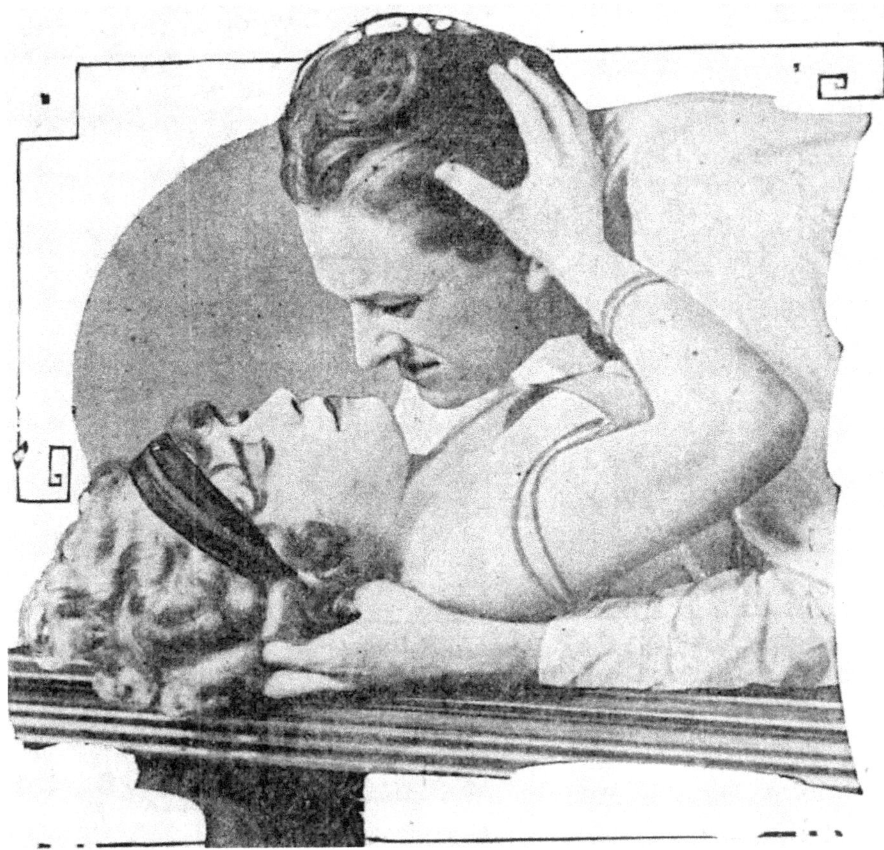

Mae West with Barry O'Neill in Sex

that showed her showbiz persona at its truest and most defined. Two years later, her play *The Constant Sinner*, was met with less success than *Diamond Lil.*

A star of big time vaudeville and the Broadway stage, a figure of controversy and notoriety, and an entertainer who was talented, engaging, beautiful, and funny, Mae West was known throughout the world by the time she was offered a movie contract by Paramount Pictures. George Raft, a friend from her stage days, was starring in a film in which one of the characters was set to be played by Texas Guinan, known as Queen of the Night Clubs for her brash manner. Guinan, however, was considered too old for the part, so Raft suggested Mae West. Paramount knew that

Ad for Diamond Lil, *a very successful show*

Mae's name would bolster the box office, and offered her the part. Mae was not interested in movies, but when told she would have some creative control, including writing her own dialog, she agreed to the role, mostly out of friendship for Raft. Mae West made her movie debut in *Night After Night,* and George Raft later stated, "She stole everything but the cameras."[6]

6 Neibaur, James L. *The George Raft Films*. BearManor Media. 2022

NIGHT AFTER NIGHT

Directed by Archie Mayo
Assistant Director: Henry Hathaway
Screenplay by Vincent Lawrence, from the story *Single Night* by Louis Bromfield, with additional dialog by Mae West.
Produced by William LeBaron
Cinematography by Ernest Haller

Cast:
George Raft . . . . Joe Anton
Constance Cummings . . . . Miss Jerry Healy
Wynne Gibson . . . . Iris Dawn
Mae West . . . . Maudie Triplett
Alison Skipworth . . . . Miss Mabel Jellyman
Roscoe Karns . . . . Leo
Louis Calhern . . . . Dick Bolton
Bradley Page . . . . Frankie Guard
Al Hill . . . . Blainey
Harry Wallace . . . . Jerky
George "Dink" Templeton . . . . Patsy
Marty Martyn . . . . Malloy
Tom Kennedy . . . . Tom the bartender
Dick Rush . . . . Bolton - Private Detective
Phillips Smalley . . . . Mr. Wilson
Dick Gordon . . . . Nightclub Patron
Carl M. Leviness . . . . Nightclub Patron
Edmund Mortimer . . . . Nightclub Patron
Patricia Farley . . . . Hatcheck Girl
Theresa Harris . . . . Ladies' Room Attendant
Bill Elliott . . . . Escort
Dennis O'Keefe . . . . Drunk Sleeping on a Table
Anderson Lawler . . . . Lonely Drunk
Leo White . . . . Kitchen Staff

Released October 30, 1932
Paramount Pictures
Running time: 73 minutes

Night After Night is notable as being George Raft's first starring role after several small parts, usually as a gangster. Audiences took notice of Raft's menacing henchman in Howard Hawks' *Scarface* and after more small roles, Raft got to bring his stoic, nuanced presence to the lead in *Night After Night,* playing Joe Anton. Anton runs a speakeasy but falls for a socialite, Miss Healy (Constance Cummings) and hires a matronly society woman, Ms. Jellyman (Alison Skipworth) to teach him proper manners. Mae West makes her film debut as Maudie, an old friend of Joe's who stops by to see him during his first dinner party with Miss Healy. Joe has also invited Ms. Jellyman to the same dinner so that she may engage him in sophisticated conversation. Maudie sits down and despite her aggressive, boorish manner, not only does she not disrupt the setting negatively, but both women find her delightful. She and the cultured Ms. Jellyman especially hit it off.

Texas Guinan was primarily not cast in the role in this film because she was considered too old for the part at 48 and was in poor health (she died the following year). One of the many impressive things about Mae West is that, while she had indeed worked on the stage since she was a child, she didn't start her movie career until she was on the cusp of 40, quite unheard of for most Hollywood leading ladies and placing her as older than most of her male costars.

Once Raft convinced Paramount to hire Mae for the role of Maudie, the movie trade magazines responded. James Cunningham stated in his Asides and Interludes column:

> Many celebrities go to Hollywood, live and work there a while, go away, and write a panning book, article or story about it. Mae West of *Diamond Lil* fame is to reverse the process. According to Paramount publicity, Miss West believes that Hollywood "has a sweetening and cleansing

Mae West is singled out in this ad for Night After Night

effect upon one's views of life." And in the same story, the company declares that the lady will play "one of her typical stage roles" in Paramount's *Night After Night*. Further on in the press announcement, Miss West is credited with being the proud author of *Sex* and *Pleasure Man* besides *Diamond Lil*.[7]

This column blurb seemed to indicate that the columnist was pretty skeptical as to how Mae West would translate to the screen. Naming her salaciously titled written works seemed to conclude that the parameters of motion pictures would be too restrictive to contain Mae West. This shows a bit of foresight in that when these restrictions were tightened after the code was enforced in 1934, the narrower parameters did become a problem.

---

7 Cunningham, James. Asides and Interludes. *Motion Picture Herald*. July 30, 1932

The trade magazine *Movie Classic* printed a feature story on Mae West's movie debut, with some information about her background on stage"

> To thousands of people who love to be shocked, the name Mae West stands for plays and novels that portray gilded and sex sin. Every new Mae West production on Broadway brings a new gasp, thrill, blush, shudder, shock, or shiver according to the nature of the theatergoer. And now this blonde author-actress, whose plays abound with seductive sinners, effeminate men, Diamond Lils, and gigolos, has come to the capital of sex. You will see her in *Night After Night* with Nancy Carroll (sic) and George Raft. And if the public likes her, you will probably see more of her. Mae thinks that several of her plays would make good motion pictures, particularly *Diamond Lil.* Time – and Mae herself – will tell.[8]

Paramount studio President Adolph Zukor stated, "No one believed that the Mae West of stage could be transferred intact to the screen."[9] But she had production head William LeBaron in her corner, as he had produced a stage show Mae was in some two decades earlier.

Mae shrewdly signed up with the William Morris Agency once Paramount came to her, figuring that if this was her only movie, she'd be paid well. Her agent arranged for a contract that offered $4000 per week with a guarantee of $20,000. This made her the highest paid person in the cast, even more than the movie's star, George Raft. William Morris also tried to book a suite at the ritzy El Royale, but the management refused the controversial star. Paramount arranged for Mae to stay in a two bedroom apartment near the studio.

---

8 Tenant, Madge. Mae West, Broadway's Most Daring Actress, Drops Into Hollywood. *Movie Classic.* September, 1932.

9 Zukor, Adolph and Dale Kramer. *The Public is Never Wrong.* NY: Putnam, 1953

Mae West had no experience with movies, but despite the studio's reticence about hiring a controversial entertainer like West, they also realized she was right for the part. West was hired and allowed to write her own dialog. In her first scene, West enters the speakeasy with a flourish and when the hat check girl exclaims, "Goodness, what lovely diamonds," West famously replies "Goodness had nothing to do with it dearie." This was her introduction to cinema, and curious moviegoers who wanted to know about this Mae West stage performer they had read about, were both shocked and tickled by the "goodness" line in her first appearance. Nearly every critic reviewing the movie made note of it. Mae told reporter Wood Soanes:

> I was ready to turn round and go home when I saw my part In *Night After Night*. I had come out here to be a star, and here I was playing a small part. Then I made up my mind to play the role for all it was worth. That's the way I got ahead in this business, taking my roles and building them up; that's the way I became a playwright rewriting material. It's impossible for authors to write material that suits me. So, I take what they prepare and fix it to suit myself. That's what I did with *'Night After Night*. I took the part, fixed the lines, added a few gags and played it to the hilt.[10]

The studio initially did not want Mae to do any rewrites. She might have had experience, but her work was too controversial for movies, even in the pre-code era. Mae was already under contract and being paid while the production was being prepared, and had already received the $20,000 before shooting began. She threatened to return to New York, so the studio allowed her to do a rewrite with the understanding that her first scene would be shot according to the original script, and with her own reworked dialog. The best scene would determine how they would continue. Mae agreed. According to Adolph Zukor: "She directed herself

---

10 Mae West Gives Film Capital Exhibitions as Smasher of Traditions. *Oakland Tribune.* December 11, 1932

Mae West and George Raft

according to her own script and ideas. Plainly, her own character-ization was better."[11] Mae was allowed to rewrite her dialog, and was given an added $16,000 as a writer's fee.

The reviewer in *The New York Daily News* called out Mae West's performance while praising Raft and Constance Cummings:

> Besides the smooth performances given by George Raft
> and Constance Cummings, the picture sponsors the film
> debut of Mae West, who, like Jimmy Durante, has the

11 Zukor, Adolph and Dale Kramer. *The Public is Never Wrong.* NY: Put-nam, 1953

sort of personality that clicks on her first appearance in a scene. Her part in *Night After Night* isn't a big one, but she dominates every scene she's in, even when she is playing against such a veteran scene-stealer as Alison Skipworth, who does more than her bit to make the picture a howling success.[12]

Other reviewers also took time to praise Mae West in her film debut. *The Los Angeles Evening Post-Record* stated: "The famous Diamond Lil has an elastic sense of humor, a bouncing breeziness, and a hard boiled gallantry." Meanwhile, the trades offered comments from exhibitors who showed *Night After Night* in their theaters, with statements like, "Mae West is a knockout" and "Mae West caused the most favorable comments from the patrons."

Finally, those who reviewed the film in more recent times also found Mae West's debut remarkable. The review for *Time Out* stated:

> It seems strange to find the stately Mae West playing a jolly character called Maudie Triplett, and even stranger to find her fourth in the cast list, but after all this was her first film. Her scenes are few, yet she throws so much into them that the leading players in this comedy drama (cool Constance Cummings and icy George Raft) momentarily fade into oblivion[13]

Film critic and historian Laura Grieve reviewed the blu ray release of *Night After Night* and wrote about Mae's performance:

> …right in the middle of dinner is when Maudie (West) appears back in Joe's life and upsets the apple cart…but, hilariously, the earthy Maudie and the refined Miss Jellyman hit it off and become friends. There's a scene where Maudie asks Miss Jellyman to join her in business and Miss Jellyman is flattered but feels she's clearly too old for what she *thinks* Maudie's business is…it turns out her

---

12 Night After Night review. *The New York Daily News.* October 29, 1932
13 Night After Night review. *Time Out.* September 10, 2012

impression is not exactly correct. Both ladies add some excellent comedy to the movie.[14]

The stuffy Hollywood brass who attended the film's premiere met West's performance with laughter and applause, and so did preview audiences throughout the country. Paramount realized Mae West's worth and offered her a lucrative contract that allowed her a level of creative control that was very rarely allowed by any of the major studios of the time. Mae West was hardly bowled over by her film debut, and mostly did it as a lark, as well as a favor to her friend George Raft (a friendship that continued until they both died, two days apart, in 1980). But the lucrative contract and creative control intrigued Mae West, so she signed to do four films for Paramount. And she then went right to work at adapting *Diamond Lil* for the screen.

14 Night After Night review. *Laura's Miscellaneous Musings*. June 22, 2021

SHE DONE HIM WRONG

Directed by Lowell Sherman
Screenplay by Harvey F. Thew and John Bright from the play *Diamond Lil* by Mae West
Produced by William LeBaron
Cinematography by Charles Lang
Film Editing by Alexander Hall

Songs:
I Wonder Where My Easy Rider's Gone
Written by Ralph Rainger

A Guy What Takes His Time
Written by Ralph Rainger

Frankie and Johnny
Music by Bert Leighton and Frank Leighton

Cast:
Mae West . . . . Lady Lou
Cary Grant . . . . Captain Cummings
Owen Moore . . . . Chick Clark
Gilbert Roland . . . . Serge Stanieff
Noah Beery . . . . Gus Jordan
David Landau . . . . Dan Flynn
Wade Boteler . . . . Dan's Pal
Rafaela Ottiano . . . . Russian Rita
Dewey Robinson . . . . Spider Kane
Rochelle Hudson . . . . Sally
Tammany Young . . . . Chuck Connors
Fuzzy Knight . . . . Rag Time Kelly
Grace La Rue . . . . Frances

Robert Homans . . . . .Doheney
Louise Beavers . . . . .Pearl
James Eagles. . . . . .Pete
Aggie Herring . . . . .Mrs. Flaherty
Lee Kohlmar . . . . .Jacobson
Tom McGuire . . . . .Mike - Lou's Coachman
Harry Wallace . . . . .Steak McGarry
Tom Kennedy. . . . . .Big Bill - Bartender
Al Hill .Barfly
Arthur Housman . . . . .Barfly
Frank Mills. . . . . .Barfly
Billy Bletcher . . . . .Singing Waiter
Lee Phelps . . . . .Singing Waiter
Harry Warren. . . . . .Waiter
Fred Santley . . . . .The Tenor
Billy B. Van. . . . . .Pianist
Mary Gordon. . . . . .Cleaning Lady
Michael Mark . . . . .Janitor
Heinie Conklin . . . . .Street Cleaner
Frank Moran . . . . .Framed Convict
Fern Emmett . . . . .Woman in Conversation
Ellinor Vanderveer . . . . .Well-Wisher in Audience
Ernie Adams . . . . .Man in Audience
Leo White . . . . .Pedestrian Tipping Hat to Lou
Florence Wix . . . . .Disapproving Passerby
Jack Carr. . . . . .Patron Who Hits His Girl
Mike Donlin . . . . .Tout
Harold Entwistle . . . . .Bit

Released January 27, 1933
Paramount Pictures
Running time: 66 minutes

Ad for She Done Him Wrong

Paramount had already obtained the rights to film *Diamond Lil* in 1931 before Mae West ever considered Hollywood. The studio planned to make it their own way with one of their own stars, despite the fact that Production Code enforcer Will Hays stated that such a film could never be approved. When a starring vehicle was needed for the newly signed Mae West, the already purchased *Diamond Lil* seemed to be an obvious choice.

In November of 1932, Mae worked with screenwriters Harvey Thew and John Bright to rework the play for the screen. The script carefully changes Mae's character name to Lady Lou, adds new material by Thew and Bright, and rewrites the more risqué lines. West actually enjoyed the creative process of disguising the more blatant lines to sneaky innuendo. She realized that with her delivery, these rewritten lines could be even funnier.

James Wingate had been a member of the censorship board since 1926 and was currently serving as a liaison between the studios and Will Hays. Paramount submitted the script to Wingate under the title *Lady Lou*. Respectful of filmmakers' creativity, Wingate admitted to Hays that he realized *Lady Lou* was actually *Diamond Lil*, but believed they had rewritten it satisfactorily for cinema. Unconvinced, Will Hays made an appointment to meet with Paramount head Adolph Zukor. Speaking in-person to Zukor and other studio heads, Hays tried in vain to convince Paramount to drop their plans to film *Diamond Lil*. He did, however, arrange for some concessions, which included editing the songs and making absolutely no reference to *Diamond Lil* in the publicity. By the time these were all worked out, the film, now titled *She Done Him Wrong*, was already in production.

Paramount was experiencing financial difficulties and needed the box office boost that a Mae West film promised. While the director was veteran Lowell Sherman, Mae's creative control allowed her a lot of clout. She had a strong say in casting the film, including friends like Owen Moore, Noah Beery, and Gilbert Roland, as well as Rafaela Ottiano, who had been in the original stage production. She wrote a part in the script for Louise Beavers, who

Cary Grant and Mae West

was an already established Black film actress who specialized in playing domestics. Mae wanted to give work to Black actors and made an effort to hire them for all of her productions. While the Black actors in her movies are definitely still in subservient roles to the white characters, there is a playful and easy camaraderie between West and Beavers here that causes them to appear closer to friends than boss and maid.

One role Mae had difficulty casting was Captain Cummings. The studio offered her several actors whom they had under contract, but Mae was not satisfied with any of them. The role was given to an up-and-coming actor known as Cary Grant. In order to expedite filmmaking as well as cut costs, Mae came up with the idea to rehearse one week before shooting. She also limited the scenes so fewer sets would be needed, another cost-saving tactic.

Lady Lou (Mae West) is a singer in a New York City Bowery bar during the 1890s. The owner of the saloon, Gus Jordan (Noah Beery) considers her a featured attraction because she brings in customers, and is also smitten, giving her gifts of jewelry. In order to afford these gifts, Gus dabbles in criminal activities, including counterfeiting, prostitution, and a pickpocketing network that he manages. His accomplices include Russian Rita (Rafaela Ottiano) and her lover Sergei Stanieff (Gilbert Roland). Dan Flynn (David Landau) is one of Lou's many past men. He tries to reveal Gus's criminal behavior to Lou, and when she doesn't respond, he threatens her. Meanwhile, the handsome young director of a nearby mission, Captain Cummings (Cary Grant), is hovering around. Lou is attracted to him, but Gus is concerned that Cummings might hurt his bar's business by reforming his patrons. Neither realizes he is actually a federal agent. Lou's boyfriend Chick Clark (Owen Moore) is currently in prison and hears that Lou has betrayed him. She goes to the prison to claim she has been true to him, and he threatens to kill her if she betrays him. He escapes from prison, finds Lou in her dressing room at the bar, and starts to strangle her, but his love for her is so strong he can't do it. Later a fight between Lou and Rita, due to a diamond Lou receives from Sergei, ends with Lou accidentally stabbing Rita. She has her loyal bodyguard Spider (Dewey Robinson) dispose of the body. She then has him bring Chick to her room while she performs her song on stage. During her song number, she nods to Dan to go up to her room, where Chick shoots and kills him. The gunshot causes a raid and Cummings, revealing himself as a federal agent, arrests Gus, Sergei, and Chick. While they are taken away in a paddy wagon, Cummings drives Lou away in a horse-drawn carriage and puts an engagement ring on her finger.

One small portion of the narrative includes Rochelle Hudson as Sally, who wanders into the saloon and is taken in by a sympathetic Lou who immediately realizes Sally's problem.

Sally: How did you know there was a man?

Lady Lou: There always is. It takes two to get one in trouble. What was he? Married?

Sally: Yes, but I didn't know.

Owen Moore and Mae West

Lady Lou: Makes no difference to me whether you did or not. Men's all alike, married or single. It's their game. I happen to be smart enough to play it their way. You'll come to it. When men go wrong, women go right after them.

Sally: You know everything about me.

Lady Lou: I wouldn't say that, but I am observant.

Rochelle Hudson would later recall the Mae West "makes you feel that you have an important part, even though she is the star."[15]

Cary Grant, however, reacted differently to having appeared in this film early in his career. Mae West would often claim that she

---

15 Tucker, David C. *Rochelle Hudson: A Biography and Career Record.* Jefferson, NC: McFarland, 2023

discovered Grant and put him in the movie, igniting his career. According to West, she happened to see unknown Cary Grant walking around the Paramount lot and said to her producer, "If he can talk, I'll take him." In fact, Grant had already appeared in eight features prior to *She Done Him Wrong,* including such notable titles as *Blonde Venus* with Marlene Dietrich, *Devil and the Deep* with Gary Cooper and Charles Laughton, and *Merrily We Go To Hell* with Fredric March. Grant even had played starring roles in the films *Hot Saturday* and *Madame Butterfly.* He was already being groomed as a leading man by the studio when he was cast in *She Done Him Wrong.* Furthermore, Grant claimed that he and Mae West had already known each other from Broadway years earlier.

It is notable that Mae West doesn't make her first appearance in *She Done Him Wrong* until almost ten minutes has elapsed, which is nearly one-sixth of the entire film's running time. However, this allows her character's reputation and anticipation for her arrival to build up before she makes her entrance. *She Done Him Wrong* is sustained by Mae West's dialog, her wry casual comments that are often edgy and always funny. While they seem quite tame in the 21st century, even in the pre-code era of 1933 they raised eyebrows. Certainly, the most famous line in *She Done Him Wrong* is often misquoted as "Come up and see me sometime." In fact, what Lady Lou says to Captain Cunningham is, "I always did like a man in a uniform. That one fits you grand. Why don't you come up some time and see me?" However, that line is earthy enough for American cinema in the early 1930s. And when Cummings asks Lou, "Haven't you ever met a man who made you happy?" And she responds, "Sure I have, lots of times," movie audiences were both shocked and titillated. "You bad girl," says Cummings. "You'll find out," replies Lou.

Mae's creative control extended to the designing of her gowns, and she worked closely with Edith Head, a Paramount costumer who was already considered one of the finest in Hollywood. West and Head worked beautifully together; Edith being impressed

Rafaela Ottiano and Mae West

by Mae's knowledge of how to best present herself. They would remain friends to the end of their lives.

This collaborative spirit did not extend to the film's director. Lowell Sherman was a veteran actor and filmmaker, who today is perhaps best known as having starred in *What Price Hollywood?* (1932), which is the first movie version of *A Star is Born* and the basis of every subsequent version of that story. During the Hollywood studio system, the director was never to be challenged by an actor, especially someone making only her second film. West, however, had very specific ideas as to how each scene would play, and while she didn't know about camera placement or editing, she was quite knowledgeable about performance and blocking. Sherman found her to be meddlesome, and even Cary Grant would later state, "She did her own thing to the detriment of all around her."[16] However, when Lowell Sherman would complain to producer William LeBaron, he found him to be in support of his new star.

---

16 McCann, Graham. *Cary Grant, A Class Apart.* NY: Columbia University Press, 1996

Newspaper ad for She Done Him Wrong

In January of 1933, Paramount was forced into receivership and were relying on this new Mae West film to help them financially. Budget costs were kept down to $200,000, a very small amount for a feature-length film, and filming concluded a few days early as well. The studio set out on a big publicity push for Mae West's first starring film, arranging previews and issuing promo pieces in the trades, including alleged interviews with West. They offered biographical details to capitalize on her titillating persona's history, and made some use of the Hays Office's negative reaction to the very idea of filming the story.

This latter tactic seemed to pay off. Negative publicity only created more interest. For instance, *She Done Him Wrong* was banned from being exhibited in Atlanta, so a theater outside of the city limits decided to show it, and it was a huge success:

Buckhead, the modern Babylon, Atlantans have gone in droves this past week, risking their presumably susceptible morals to see Miss West in *She Done Him Wrong*. This film has been placed on the index expurgatorius of the Atlanta Board of Film Review, but the public, with shocking lack of respect for the boards pronouncements, has packed the Buckhead Theater all week, so that Willis Davis, the manager, announces that *She Done Him Wrong* will be held over Monday, Tuesday and Wednesday. This irreverent column outraged all propriety by disagreeing with the Atlanta Board of Film Review and pronouncing *She Done Him Wrong* a perfectly grand entertainment. It hooted the Better Films Committee for not defending a film which has been consistently praised throughout the country, and suppressed nowhere else. Last Saturday, learning that an expurgated version of *She Done Him Wrong* was to be shown at Buckhead, we started a one-man campaign for the entire film, and induced the Paramount Exchange to release, and Mr. Willis to show, an uncut edition, contending that not one scene in the film is objectionable to anyone with a normal amount of humor and understanding.[17]

The elements featured in *She Done Him Wrong* would be taboo in a few short years once the Production Code was more sternly enforced. But during this pre-code era, the culture somehow allowed a movie containing prostitution, adultery, murder, double-entendre dialog, and songs with suggestive lyrics. Speaking of the songs, composer Ralph Rainger, later known for composing Bob Hope's theme song "Thanks For The Memory," and Jack Benny's theme song "Love in Bloom," composes two songs here. "I Wonder Where My Easy Rider's Gone" and "A Guy What Takes His Time" were both performed by Mae West, challenging the lyr-

---

17 Daniel, Frank. Diamond Lil Held Over She Done Him Wrong: Banned in Atlanta Continues Its Engagement After 'Capacity Week at the Buckhead Theater. *Atlanta Constitution*. April 16, 1933

ics to appear more suggestive than likely intended. But the show stopper is her signature tune "Frankie and Johnny." The latter song number became one of the highlights of the movie, and Mae would perform on Rudy Vallee's radio show as part of the film's promotion. West wasn't a technically great singer, but she performs the lyrics with the same saucy delivery as her dialogue, which makes those numbers memorable and entertaining.

Reviews were mostly positive, but *Variety* felt that Paramount was rushing Mae West into leading roles before she was ready, and that the film had an uninteresting story and no notable names in the cast. This latter claim is easily disproven, as Noah Beery, Owen Moore, and Gilbert Roland were quite well known, and Cary Grant was an up-and-coming talent at the time. *The New York Daily News* stated:

> The atmosphere of the old Bowery is right there in
> *She Done Him Wrong*, Mae West's bolt of celluloid art
> which is keeping the customers giggling. The movie is
> suggested by *Diamond Lil*, which served the blonde,
> buxom Mae as a feverish footlight vehicle. But the film
> is somewhat toned down being just about as naughty as
> the censor's scissors permitted. Mae gives us Lady Lou,
> bedecked with finery and jewels, who sings risque ditties
> in a Bowery honky-tonk. Lots of action, much color-
> ful background, tough-mug acting and snappy direction
> by Lowell Sherman plus songs by Mae, warbled in her
> inimitable manner make *She Done Him Wrong* strong for
> the box-office.[18]

The Los Angeles Times was also supportive of the film and, in opposition to the perspective offered by *Variety*, respected the supporting cast:

> It is a rough, raucous, bawdy picture, Franky and Johnny
> prurient but so vitalized, so authoritatively and effectively
> staged and acted, that it becomes one of the more exciting

---

18 Thirer, Irene. She Done Him Wrong review. *The New York Daily News.*
    February 10, 1933

Trade ad for She Done Him Wrong

exhibits of recent weeks. It is indeed almost spectacular in its braggadocio, in its brash disregard of whatever rules still remain to guide the movie producers in their emboldened advance along a path which once used to be known forbiddingly as primrose -- a fact which is proved, curiously and inversely enough, in the scene which is supposed to evidence a belated respect for the conventions. This is that one, the last, in which Capt. Cummings suddenly and unaccountably affiances himself to the lady known as Lou. Mae West is the whole show -- an incredible throwback to corseted grandeur and proportions heroically amplified, plumed of hat and furred of gown, aglitter from head to foot with diamonds that flash in the sun-arcs. Sincere only in her insincerities, she knocks 'em dead, one and all, with a stare and a honeyed word. It represents a definite progression in the directorial efforts of Lowell Sherman; a conspicuously well done reproduction of "a lusty, brawling, florid decade." Notably good performances are achieved by virtually all members of the company....[19]

The movie trade magazines responded favorably as well, with feature stories about this stage presence who was a newcomer to films. A feature in *Silver Screen* stated:

Well, Aunt Emma can keep the birds and the bees. She can get a thrill out of their nesting and having for we don't need them anymore. Mae West has torn the veil from hypocrisy and come right out into the open (well almost) on this Sex business. Hollywood has been smirking and giggling over Jean Harlow's slipping gowns, Marlene Dietrich's pants and Ernst Lubitsch's bed for months and years now and feeling so naughtily abandoned. Yet it took a blonde from Brooklyn to grab Sex up out of the mire and put it on a paying basis. And does Sex pay!

19 Scheuer, Phillip K. She Done Him Wrong review. *The Los Angeles Times.* January 31, 1933

> If there's any doubt in your mind, just examine the box
> office receipts for *She Done Him Wrong*. Just look at *She
> Done Him Wrong*. You probably have three times or more.
> No movie star in Hollywood has ever had such a personal
> triumph. The picture has already netted over two million
> dollars and it isn't through yet.[20]

Meanwhile, a feature on Mae West in the trade magazine *Motion Picture* compared her favorably with Greta Garbo and Marlene Dietrich.

> Mae West is the first and real Waterloo the Garbo and
> Dietrich schools of sultry, languorous, erotic emotions.
> Because she has made them appear slightly foolish, as
> if they didn't know how to get a kick out of life. And
> whether the vivid and voluptuous, electric and elegant.
> Any red-blooded he-man can understand Mae. She
> speaks his language and her figure speaks for itself. He
> becomes her man, but he can do her no wrong. His lush,
> full-blooded sister understands her too, and likewise
> becomes her pal. That's why American is flocking to see
> Mae on the screen. The movie audiences have become
> curves conscious again and Mae is leading the way. What
> a woman![21]

She Done Him Wrong was a major box office success throughout the country, and the studio benefited from a film that grossed over $2 million against its low $200,000 budget. It was held over, brought back for second engagements, and made Mae West a top level movie star with only her second film appearance and first movie in the leading role. This success also proved that Mae's popularity wasn't limited to men only. Women found her compellingly triumphant, and lines like "You can be had," and "Come up and see me some time," became catchphrases in the American lexicon. Despite the latter quote being a misquote, Mae accepted it as such and even had a welcome mat created with the phrase,

20 Keats, Patricia. Sex is Beautiful. *Silver Screen*. November, 1933
21 Schallert, Elza. Go West If You're an Adult. *Motion Picture*. May, 1933

which she placed at the door of her dressing room. The line, as misquoted, would be used in her next film, *I'm No Angel*, which also featured Cary Grant.

A female movie fan from Chicago wrote a letter to the editor of *Picture Play* magazine offering a good overall representation of how women were reacting to Mae West:

> Recently I saw Mae West in *She Done Him Wrong*. Say, there's a girl who can show these demure ingenues, sophisticated women of the world, and simpering dowagers a few artful tricks. There can only be one Mae West. Her rich, throaty voice has that indescribable quality which makes one listen fascinated. She liver her part so realistically that one was in sympathy with her in spite of her hard exterior. It certainly was soft on the eyes to see a woman that actually looked like one instead of an emaciated creature strutting her bones before the camera. All in all, it was a refreshing picture and I hope Mae is in Hollywood to stay.[22]

She Done Him Wrong was not only a major box office hit, it received an Academy Award nomination for Best Picture (then called Outstanding Production). With its short 66 minute running time, *She Done Him Wrong* remains the shortest feature to receive such a nomination. Exhibitors wrote in the trades to indicate how their audiences responded to the film: "I played this to adults only and was glad on two counts." "Risque and raw but they all liked it here." However, there were also negative comments, such as one theater owner in North Dakota who stated:

> Mae West may be a wow in some spots but out here in the sticks she doesn't mean a thing. We've never seen her on the legitimate stage and to our patrons she can't get by on her reputation. As a result, we pulled her movie after the first night.[23]

---

22 Lorenz, Alice. Mae West Soft on the Eyes. *Picture Play.* August, 1933
23 What the Picture Did For Me. *Motion Pictured Herald.* November 18, 1933

Mae West's first starring film was a success at every level, and even the negative publicity generated by those who protested the content of *She Done Him Wrong* inadvertently generated even more interest, increasing its box office. Mae West understood from experience that this sort of notoriety could be good for the film, and welcomed this reaction. *She Done Him Wrong* was instrumental in saving Paramount from bankruptcy, and thus the studio was quite eager to get Mae West's second starring film into production as quickly as possible.

I'M NO ANGEL

Directed by Wesley Ruggles
Screenplay by Mae West from her own story
Produced by William LeBaron
Cinematography by Lou Tover
Film Editing by Otto Lovering

Music
They Call Me Sister Honky-Tonk
Music by Harvey Brooks
Lyrics by Gladys DuBois and Ben Ellison

That Dallas Man
Music by Harvey Brooks
Lyrics by Gladys DuBois and Ben Ellison

I Found a New Way to Go to Town
Music by Harvey Brooks
Lyrics by Gladys DuBois and Ben Ellison

I Want You, I Need You
Music by Harvey Brooks
Lyrics by Ben Ellison

I'm No Angel
Music by Harvey Brooks
Lyrics by Gladys DuBois and Ben Ellison

Cast:
Mae West . . . . Tira
Cary Grant . . . . Jack Clayton
Gregory Ratoff . . . . Benny Pinkowitz

Edward Arnold . . . . Big Bill Barton
Ralf Harolde. . . . . Slick Wiley
Kent Taylor. . . . . Kirk Lawrence
Gertrude Michael. . . . . Alicia Hatton
Russell Hopton . . . . The Barker Flea Madigan
Dorothy Peterson . . . . Thelma
William B. Davidson . . . . The Chump Ernest Brown
Gertrude Howard. . . . . Beulah Thortndyke
Libby Taylor . . . . Tira's Maid
Hattie McDaniel . . . . Tira's Maid
Nat Pendleton . . . . Harry - Acrobat
George Bruggeman . . . . Omnes
Lew Kelly. . . . . Joe - Animal Keeper
Nell Craig. . . . . Mrs. Bond
Nigel De Brulier. . . . . Rajah the Fortune Teller
Irving Pichel. . . . . Bob - Clayton's Attorney
Laura Treadwell . . . . Mrs. Fletcher
Walter Walker . . . . Judge
Monte Collins . . . . Sailor at Circus
Ray Cooke . . . . Sailor at Circus
Morrie Cohan . . . . Bartons Chauffeur
Eddie Borden. . . . . Sideshow Spectator
Tom London . . . . Sideshow Spectator
Mahlon Hamilton . . . . Sideshow Spectator
Lee Phelps . . . . Sideshow Spectator
Duke York . . . . Sideshow Spectator
Larry Steers . . . . Lawyer at Courtroom
                                            Defense Table
Edward Hearn . . . . Court Clerk
Ronald R. Rondell . . . . Courtroom Spectator
Carl M. Leviness . . . . Courtroom Spectator
 Edmund Mortimer . . . . Courtroom Spectator
Dennis O'Keefe . . . . Courtroom Reporter
Robert McKenzie. . . . . Man at Rooming House
Jack Pennick. . . . . Carny on spotlight
Bobby Barber . . . . Man In Crowd

Released October 6, 1933
Paramount Pictures
Running time: 87 minutes

Mae West's popularity had been ignited by *Night After Night* and became quite huge after the release of her first starring film. The success of *She Done Him Wrong*, from box office dollars to being nominated for a Best Picture Oscar, resulted in a great deal of publicity filling newspapers to satisfy a public eager for more information about this captivating new movie star.

A syndicated series of biographical features came out of the *Los Angeles Times* and appeared in newspapers throughout the country. Presented in several parts, these stories traced Mae's life from childhood, through her early stage work, her Broadway success, and subsequent controversies. This activity was well known in New York, and perhaps also pretty well known in California, but the southern and midwestern newspaper readers only had a general knowledge of West's exploits before appearing in hit movies. They saw her suggestive performances, and read some cursory accounts of her past, but now they were able to get a fuller understanding of who she was and from where she had come.

Along with this series of features, newspapers were filled with syndicated articles where Mae talked about how to get a man, discussed her fashion sense, even her size and shape. Articles let readers know that Mae was not a slight woman, and was rather buxom, but also quite short. West herself stated that 119 pounds was her best weight, but did not specifically admit to being under five feet tall.

One of the more amusing features regarding Mae had appeared in *Screenland*. A writer from that magazine visited the set of *I'm No Angel* and asked Mae to list her Ten Get-Your-Man Commandments. This is what she came up with:

Ad for I'm No Angel

1). Be Available – contrive so he's aware of your presence

2). Be Self-Sufficient – let him know you're hot, but let him start the blaze himself

3). Be Beautiful – because temptation at first sight saves a heck of a lot of time.

4). Be Elemental – don't give 'em English accents when they crave a gal who don't pretend

5). Be Entertaining – the fastest way to register is to feed a man's vanity, not his stomach

6). Be Feminine – in ways and dress that allows you a thousand and one tricks

7). Be Sophisticated – a woman who can add two and two seldom has unhappy days and lonely nights

8). Be Popular – ten dates on the string are worth more than one on a davenport, and besides the reserves spur on the most ardent

9). Be Changeable – and you're sure never to be handed that "a book's no good once I have read it" line.

10). Be Selfish – so you won't be sorry.[24]

Mae West continued to stir up controversy and interest

Of course, there were articles that responded negatively to West's stardom, usually in the form of letters to editors or columnists by typical religious reformers who were taken aback by the sexuality inherent in her stage and screen persona. One lengthy letter from

---

24 Mae West Tells How to Get a Man. *Screenland* December 1933

what appears to be a typical moviegoer of the period claimed that West was not "marriage material." This appeared in the November 2, 1933 edition of Cynthia Grey's advice column:

Dear Cynthia:

It seems strange that nobody has written to you about Mae West. It seems to me every woman and almost every man in town is talking about her. A group of us were discussing her at lunch the other day. We were just four ordinary women not too young and not too old .Two of us were married and two were not. We are reasonably attractive. We couldn't agree about Mae West. One of the girls said that any woman could act like she does on the screen and that she could have the men fall for her as they do for Mae West. She contended that the average woman had too much self-respect to "lower in that way." The rest of us disagreed with her .The charm or attraction or sex appeal that Mae West has isn't part of the make-up of every woman. The West type is a special type. On the screen the men fall for her like flies for a jar of honey. But in real life it is different. The average man doesn't want to marry a woman like that. He may become infatuated with her but he seldom falls in love with her. He almost never asks her to marry him. She represents a type of cold cal-culating voluptuousness that is amusing but repellant to the average male. Actually, the West type would frighten away far more men than she would attract. When a man marries he wants a wife whom he can trust. He wants the one woman who belongs to him and only to him. He doesn't want to take someone who invites the attention of every man she meets. Men fall in love with innocence, gentleness, kindness, and charm. A woman with those qualities gets a husband far more quickly than one who flamboyantly flaunts sex from the housetops. A snappy

comeback is worse than a crooked nose and a hairlip so
far as attracting men is concerned.[25]

This letter is quite a fascinating period piece, an interesting window into a past culture where women expected to "belong" to men and believed an independent wisecracking woman like Mae West is only a superficial attraction. Perhaps this indicates that West's showbiz persona generated some insecurity in "ordinary women not too young and not too old" who were "reasonably attractive."

A much more amusing encounter occurred when it was discovered an "ordinary woman" living in Iowa named May West kept getting fan mail from moviegoers attempting to contact the star. When Mae heard about it, she made arrangements to fly May West out to Hollywood for a screening of *I'm No Angel* at Grauman's Chinese Theater. Upon first meeting her almost-namesake, Mae West stated, "so you're the gal who's been readin' my mail!"[26]

The success of *She Done Him Wrong*, along with all of the publicity, allowed Mae West's star to rise so quickly, her next Paramount feature was planned to be longer, and with more depth and substance. And this time Mae West was credited alone for the story and screenplay.

Cary Grant was back as leading man, and this time Wesley Ruggles was hired to direct. Ruggles was a Paramount director noted for getting along well with his actors. His patience was considered just the right type to direct someone like Mae West who asserted a great deal of creative control. The credits even point out this level of control, stating "Story, Screenplay and All Dialogue by MAE WEST," her name in all capital letters and written large. Much smaller, and beneath her name are credits "With Suggestions by Lowell Brentano," and "Continuity by Harlan Thompson." Mae West could write a screenplay, just as she could write a play, but there were structural things for which a newcomer to cinema would need some assistance. That is where someone like Brentano

---

25 Mae West's Methods Won't Land Husband, Says Reader. *The Spokane Press.* November 2, 1933

26 May West guest of Mae West at Chinese Theater. *Los Angeles Daily News.* October 25, 1933

Trade ad for I'm No Angel

or Thompson would come in. This level of creative control, with credit, could only be given to someone whose work saved a studio from bankruptcy.

Mae West plays Tira, a major attraction at Big Bill's Wonder Show. While she performs, her boyfriend Slick (Ralf Harolde) picks the pockets of the distracted crowd. Tira invites one of her fans, Ernest Brown (William Davidson) to her apartment. She is just about to get him to invest money in the show when Slick walks in and confronts him. Tira attempts to wise Slim up to her scheme, but Brown figures it out and threatens to go to the cops. Slick hits Brown on the head with a bottle, and believes he has killed him. They put the body in the hall, but Brown is revived and does go to the cops. Slick is arrested and Tira asks Big Bill (Edward Arnold) for money to hire a lawyer (Gregory Ratoff). Bill agrees, only if Tira performs with the lions including sticking her head in the lion's mouth. Desperate, she reluctantly agrees. This causes her popularity to increase and she goes from side show to part of the main program. Her increasing popularity has her performing in New York where wealthy playboy Kirk Lawrence

(Kent Taylor) falls for her and starts buying her expensive gifts, despite being engaged to Alicia Hatton (Gertrude Michael). Kirk's wealthier cousin Jack Clayton (Cary Grant) goes to see Tira in order to break up her romance with Kirk, but falls for her himself. They eventually become engaged, but Big Bill, not wanting to lose his main attraction, creates a scheme with Slick, who has just been released from prison, to be in Tira's apartment wearing a robe when Jack comes to call, while Tira is distracted and not at home. Jack calls off the engagement and Tira sues in court for breach of promise. During the trial, Tira manages to charm the judge and the jury when she takes it upon herself to cross-examine all witnesses. Jack agrees to give her a settlement. She tears up his check and they reconcile.

Director Wesley Ruggles opens *I'm No Angel* with a nice establishing shot presenting a crowded, active carnival where "Tira the Incomparable" is the star attraction. Several extras are jammed together so that there is no negative space in the frame. Even the closer shots of Tira coming out on stage has her bracketed by several men, Ruggles offering cutaways to the crowd gawking with obvious intent. It is the sort of sexual undercurrent that set Mae's film's apart and resulted in protests from fringe types; this reaction only creating more interest from the general moviegoer. The director's shot composition in this opening scene is quite impressive, with medium shots showing Tira on stage with the crowd framing her, and a band in the lower foreground.

West's character of Tira is established quickly, with her benevolence toward a woman, a lonely carnival acquaintance, who is given a gift of a necklace after admiring it. While showing her various trinkets, she points out photos on the inside of her costume trunk – men who had given her the various baubles and beads. Several male carnival performers approach her as she walks through, showing her easy popularity. She consults a fortune teller friend, who states, "I see a man in your life." Disappointed, she asks, "What, only one?"

Russell Hopton, Mae West

When she is in the room of Ernest Brown, playing records and gyrating about to the music, she gets him increasingly more excited with the intention of benefiting from his wealth and weak character.

Tira: By the way, honey, you married or single?

Ernest Brown: Married five times.

Tira: Five times? Wedding bells must sound like an alarm clock to you.

William Davidson plays this beautifully, coming closer, nuzzling her neck, and spouting lines like "you're given me the time of my life, baby!" When Tira comments on his wealth, he says, loftily, "that's nothin.'" She starts to get him interested in investing with the carnival when Slick busts in and wrecks the scheme. The man

Edward Arnold, Mae West, Russell Hopton

figures out the scheme and that's when the assault takes place and the man is suspected to have died.

When Brown lives, and Slick gets picked up, Mae shows her innate acting talent as Tira is genuinely concerned about being implicated in what she still believes is murder. Her pleading with Big Bill to give her money to get away is brilliantly played. Mae West realizes that while Tira must be concerned, even to the point of being scared, she still needs to maintain her cool. West succeeds in balancing these emotions perfectly.

The cinematic approach is even more impressive in a scene where Tira must take the place of the lion tamer. Of course, Mae West does not actually stick her head in a lion's mouth, the editing and effects present it quite well, especially for 1933. Ruggles shoots closeups of the lions, looking menacing as they enter the cage, and process shots using double exposure make it looks like

Mae is playing opposite them (the lions are slightly softer focus than her image).

Tira seems to have more in common and a better connection with her maid than with the society people that come back stage to visit after the lion act. When she overhears a haughty society woman berating her outside her dressing room, she opens the door and pours water on the woman's back. Coming back in the house, she says to Beulah, "did you hear that broad berating me?

A montage shows Tira's relationship with Kirk Lawrence, from the sending of expensive gifts to the opening of an account from which she can draw money and purchase items herself. Her table shows several trinkets with framed men's pictures by each, presenting who had given her which item. She warbles part of a blues number as she is surrounded by Black women giving her a haircut, manicure, and pedicure. They engage in risqué dialog with her, one of them stating, "I'm just crazy about dark men," and when one asks Tira if she is a one woman man, she replies, "one man at a time." Their impromptu dancing together as Mae sings shows the easy camaraderie that is the counterpart to her being something of an outcast among the society people. Entertainment reporter Bobby Rivers stated in an essay:

> When a Mae West character, who was usually from the wrong side of the tracks like a lot of us minority folks were in the movies, made it to the big time and had domestic help, the Black maids were never treated like second class citizens. Her Black maids were treated more like girlfriends. Watch when Tira relaxes with her maids, tries on new clothes and sings "I Found A New Way To Go To Town." Those gals are having a good time![27]

It was pretty much unheard of at the time for Black characters to be given dialogue like they are here—in that conversation, they are expressing sexual desires in a way that any other movie would never have allowed.

---

27   Rivers, Bobby. Mae West in I'm No Angel. Bobby Rivers TV. July 3, 2014

Kirk sees her as a novelty, and Tira takes advantage of the conde-scension. But her confrontation with Alicia is pure conflict:

Alicia Hatton: I suppose you know why I'm here

Tira: Hardly! You see, I'm a lion tamer not a mind reader.

Alicia Hatton: Then it might refresh you to know that I'm Kurt's fiancé.

Tira: There's nothing refreshing about that.

Alicia Hatton: It's perfectly obvious what your intentions are. Kirk has lots of money, and….

Tira: Now wait a minute. Whatever you're thinking you're wrong. I only like him like a brother.

Alica Hatton: You're a liar!

Tira: Say listen you, a better dame than you once called me a liar and they had to sew her up in twelve different places!

When Alicia tries to pay her off, Tira physically shoves her out the door, and then struts over to her maid, stating, "Beulah, peel me a grape!" This would become one of Mae West's most famous lines.

When Slick is released from prison and comes to see Tira, she appreciates his having taken the rap for her, which is why she gives him some money and sets up a job for him with Barton. She then mutters, "he would show up now." It is a telling piece of dialog and shows Mae West the writer's cleverness in utilizing the characters in the narrative at the right time.

Tira's first encounter with Jack Clayton shows an obvious attrac-tion the plays out with an underlying awkwardness. West and Cary Grant show the same chemistry they had exhibited in *She Done Him Wrong*. Tira's clever manipulation of two different handsome, wealthy men shows her power. Director Ruggles uses a closeup of a newspaper's society blurb indicating her engagement to Clayton, and the fact that his cousin Kirk Lawrence had once "spent a mess of G's on her." At one point when Tira is talking to

Cary Grant, Mae West

Clayton she uses another of Mae's most notable lines, "When I'm good, I'm very good, and when I'm bad I'm better."

When Big Bill and Slick mess up the engagement they pay off a chauffeur to claim car trouble, keeping Tira away from her penthouse. He states, "I'm doing my best," to which she replies, "Then try doing your worst." Mae West's acting is impressive when Tira really lets down her emotional guard when she finds that Jack has called off the engagement, quietly asking Beulah to leave.

The courtroom scene is a strong conclusion, as Tira's easy manner and sarcasm delights the court and the judge. It is especially amusing when Tira takes over the questioning as her past men are put on the stand, from the first chump Ernest Brown, and including both Kirk Lawrence and Jack Clayton. She unravels Brown by having him admit to his five wives, one of which he had been married to when he was at her apartment. When Kirk tells the prosecution he felt he had been played, she cross-examines by having him admit he had been engaged to Alicia, and that he willingly gave her gifts that she had not specifically asked for. Tira has no

Ralf Harolde, Mae West

problem cross-examining Slick, who had been in jail, and has a criminal background.

It is when Beulah takes the stand and admits truthfully that Tira admitted to "falling so hard" over Jack, that "it hurt," Tira admonishes her for saying too much.

Beulah: I'm just telling the truth like you said.

Tira: Yeah, but you're telling too much of it.

Jack became more and more attracted to Tira during the proceedings, resulting in the eventual reconciliation, especially after he visits Tira and she tells him it was all a frame up. As the court proceeding ends, Tira states, "It's not the men in your life it's the life in your men," which would become another of her signature lines.

Mae West's screenplay is filled with interesting well-drawn characters, witty dialog, and keeps her at the forefront of every scene. She even draws on a noted line of dialog from *She Done*

Him Wrong. When a random juror calls her with interest, she says over the phone, "Come up and see me sometime."

I'm No Angel was a huge box office hit, breaking records at many theaters. Most bookings were held over to handle the crowds, as moviegoers came to see the film multiple times. The laughter in the audience was so loud, it would drown out some of the dialog, so people would return to catch dialog they had missed. The trade magazine *Motion Picture Daily* stated:

> *I'm No Angel* will be a box office success. Patrons are eager to see it and showmen are avidly waiting for it. Following her skyrocket rise in *She Done Him Wrong*, Mae West gyrates through *I'm No Angel*, a vivid provocative personality. Her tremendous popularity which swept the country in the wake of the repeat runs on *She Done Him Wrong*, evidences the girl's powerful pull with the cash customers. Mae West fans will surely get their money's worth from this picture.[28]

A couple of months after the release of *I'm No Angel*, newspapers reported that the men who robbed Mae a year earlier had been arrested

> Charged with robbing Mae of $20,400 in money and jewels more than a year ago; two men were under arrest today and a third was sought. Harry Voiler, one time manager the late Texas Guinan, was held in Chicago in connection with the robbery and Edward H. Triedman was held (in Los Angeles). Detroit police have been asked to search for Morris Cohen. The three were indicted by the grand jury yesterday. Chief of Police James Davis said Friedman confessed the robbery and named Voiler and Cohen as his accomplices. Voiler, who had known Miss West for several years and frequently accompanied the screen star in her automobile to the studio, was named by Friedman as the "finger and directing leader In the

---

28 Shapiro, Vic. I'm No Angel Review. *Motion Picture Daily.* October 5, 1933

robbery." For their part of the crime, Friedman said, he and Cohen were to receive $1,000 each. Friedman said the actress was robbed in front of her apartment when Miss West, her manager, J. A. Timothy, and Voiler drove up in Voiler's automobile. Two days after the robbery, the reported confession continued, Voiler gave the two men $1,000 each and took in exchange the jewels and cash from the actress.[29]

Friedman was sentenced to two years at San Quentin, Cohen was not charged, and Voiler fled to Cuba and escaped prosecution. After this incident, Mae West was assigned protection by detectives Jack Sothern and Jack Criss.

Mae West was inspired by this incident to add a jewel robbery to her next script, which she planned to call *It Ain't No Sin*. However, as 1933 became 1934, the moralists who found Mae West's movies to be objectionable made enough noise for the production code to be more stringently enforced. According to film critic and scholar Katie Carter:

> It's easy to see why Mae West and *I'm No Angel* in particular would be major factors in getting the production code enforced. Pretty much every line of dialogue West utters in the movie is racy or a double entendre, and the shots are packed with visual gags (like the photos of the men she keeps in her trunk, or how her singing is cut off in the final shot as Cary Grant moves closer to her and the screen fades to black). I think the songs were the major sticking point for the censors at the time, and some of the titles had to be altered for it to pass (like "No One Does It Like a Dallas Man" being changed to "No One Loves Me Like a Dallas Man"). One of the great things about many pre-code movies is how they were often able to deal forthrightly with women's issues, and *I'm No Angel* in particular is about female empowerment: for the entire

---

29 Two Men Seized For Robbery of Mae West, Actress, in Los Angeles. AP Syndicated story. December 5, 1933

film, Tira is pushing back against the stuffy high society class represented in a character like Alicia. She's a career woman, entertains multiple affairs at once, wears beautiful, tight gowns, and isn't afraid to voice her desires. Even in the climax, she serves as her own lawyer, something pretty unheard of for a woman at the time to do. But I think what also makes her so great in this movie is that she allows us to catch glimpses of the softer, more human side of her that isn't all bawdy behavior.

These restrictions that would affect the motion picture industry for decades to come would be especially impactful on Mae West's films. And it began with her next Paramount movie, *Belle of the Nineties*.

BELLE OF THE NINETIES

Directed by Leo McCarey
Screenplay by Mae West from her story *It Ain't No Sin*, with additional dialog by Jack Wagner
Produced by William LeBaron
Cinematography by Karl Struss
Film Editing by LeRoy Stone

Songs:
Memphis Blues
Written by W.C. Handy

My Old Flame
Music by Arthur Johnston
Lyrics by Sam Coslow

Troubled Waters
Music by Arthur Johnston
Lyrics by Sam Coslow

When a St. Louis Woman Goes Down to New Orleans
Music by Arthur Johnston
Lyrics by Sam Coslow

Cast:
Mae West . . . . Ruby Carter
Roger Pryor . . . . Tiger Kid
Johnny Mack Brown . . . . Brooks Claybourne
John Miljan . . . . Ace Lamont
Katherine DeMille . . . . Molly Brant
Duke Ellington . . . . Piano Player
James Donlan . . . . Kirby

Stuart Holmes . . . . Dirk
Harry Woods . . . . Slade
Edward Gargan . . . . Stogie
Libby Taylor . . . . Jasmine
Warren Hymer . . . . St. Louis Fighter
Benny Baker . . . . Blackie
Morrie Cohan . . . . Butch
George Reed . . . . Brother Eben
Tom Herbert . . . . Gilbert
Tyler Brooke . . . . Comedian
Eddie Borden . . . . Comedian
Fuzzy Knight . . . . Comedian
Gene Austin . . . . St. Louis Crooner
Kit Guard . . . . St. Louis Gym Mug
Charles Irwin . . . . Master of Ceremonies at
                                                St. Louis
Frank Mills . . . . New Orleans Gym Mug
Ellinor Vanderveer . . . . New Orleans Dowager
Mike Mazurki . . . . New Orleans Audience
                                                Admirer
Charles Sullivan . . . . New Orleans Audience
                                                Admirer
Walter Walker . . . . New Orleans Admirer
Dave O'Brien . . . . Shipboard Admirer
Sam McDaniel . . . . Jasmine's Admirer
Ronald R. Rondell . . . . Admirer
Carlton Griffin . . . . Admirer
James Pierce . . . . Admirer
Frank McGlynn Sr. . . . . Justice of the Peace
Frank Rice . . . . Best Man at Wedding
Sam Flint . . . . Fire Chief
Brooks Benedict . . . . Roulette Table Spectator
Kay Deslys . . . . Beef Trust Chorus Girl
Edward Hearn . . . . Croupier

Blue Washington . . . . Doorman at Sensation House
Reese Corporal. . . . . Coachman
The King's Men . . . . Troubled Waters Quartet
Lawrence Stewart. . . . . Stevedore
Paul Venerable . . . . Stevedore
Cornelius Ballard . . . . Stevedore
Mark Carnahan . . . . Stevedore
Edgar Hampton. . . . . Stevedore

Released September 21, 1934
Paramount Pictures
Running time: 73 minutes

Talking pictures, made from 1929-1934, are considered the "pre-code" era, where the production code that already existed for movies was not strictly enforced. As stated earlier, representatives like James Wingate understood and respected the creative process of cinema and restrictions were lax. This paved the way for violent gangster dramas and suggestive sexual ideas, which raised the ire of moralists. Films certainly did not have the freedoms of post-1969 and the MPAA ratings system, but there was enough to upset certain groups.

The production of this film, particularly its many run-ins with the censors, is well-documented, and reflects that while the censors had a lot of power over what was released, Mae West was still able to retain a lot of agency in how she strategized the best way to confront the censors as opposed to taking or leaving what they had to say.

As Mae was beginning work on her new screenplay, which she called *It Ain't No Sin*, several religious organizations were forming to boycott motion pictures that they deemed were not wholesome enough for the viewing audience. The most notable was the Catholic Legion of Decency, which developed an actual rating system that ranged from A-1 (acceptable for all ages) to C (condemned outright). These groups found James Wingate to be ineffective as a censor, so Will Hays replaced him with Joseph Breen, a devout Catholic who relished his power. The film industry was certainly unhappy with this sort of policing, as it not only overtook their self-regulation, but limited their creativity. But Joseph Breen's power was such that the film industry changed for the next three decades.

Mae West behind the camera

Mae West, Roger Pryor

Mae West was one of the focal points of this censorship, although in later years she claimed that Barbara Stanwyck movies like *Baby Face* and *Night Nurse* were also culprits that simply got less publicity than her films. Still, Mae finished the script for *It Ain't No Sin,* and purposely added some especially salacious dialog in an effort to distract the censors from some of the double-entendres she hoped to sneak in.

The original story features Mae as Ruby Carter, an ex-prostitute who has escaped a murder rap to eventually become a star of Burlesque. She hooks up with prizefighter Tiger Kid, but her manager breaks them up and secures her a job with Ace Lamont in New Orleans. Lamont falls for her, as does society man Brooks Clayburne, but she ends up back in the arms of Tiger, who kills Lamont. Ruby helps Tiger cover up the murder. They light his club on fire, then escape on a riverboat. "Where do we go from here?" Tiger asks. "Didn't your mother teach you anything?" is Ruby's reply.

This version was being filmed with Will Hays rep John Hammell policing the production. West's director was Leo McCarey, who had gotten his start in comedies featuring Laurel and Hardy and Charley Chase, and was used to allowing his star a lot of creative control. West especially enjoyed working with McCarey, who was supportive and collaborative throughout the production. Paramount cinematographer Karl Struss also worked on this film, adding his keen visual sense for the shots McCarey assigned. *Belle of the Nineties* is one of Mae West's most visually remarkable films with artful shots and even the use of super-imposed images to enhance one highlight scene.

Paramount took advantage of the fact that while Mae West was a controversial figure, she was also one of Hollywood's biggest stars, so they ran articles in the fan magazines complaining about how they were restricting what made her famous. For all of the moralists, Mae also had plenty of fans who liked what she did and didn't want her to change. Many readers wrote to the fan magazines, complaining about the censors trying to "make a lady out of Diamond Lil."

For her part, Mae West insisted on a closed set. She usually welcomed visitors wanting to watch her filming, but she used the jewel robbery as a ploy to insist on tighter restrictions and guards, when this was just a way to keep Breen and associates out of the way as filming progressed.

When *It Ain't No Sin* was screened for Joseph Breen, he rejected it almost completely. Even after his demanded cuts and changes were made, it was still banned in many cities after its New York premiere due to the Catholic Legion of Decency and other such groups protesting. Several love scenes had to be re-shot, as was the ending, the film now concluding with Ruby marrying Tiger. Ruby was no longer an ex-prostitute, but a hard working stage performer. The movie did not finally get full approval until the sex

Ad for Belle of the Nineties

and the criminality was either removed or heavily altered. The title was changed to *Belle of the Nineties*.

Set in the late 19th century, the story features Ruby Carter, a vaudeville star performing at a St Louis nightclub. Prizefighter Tiger Kid (Roger Pryor) is her romantic partner, but Tiger's manager Kirby (James Donlan), believes the romance is a distraction. Kirby convinces Tiger that Ruby has been cheating on him, hoping he will refocus on his training, and Tiger sends Ruby a letter breaking up with her. Heartbroken Ruby leaves the area and accepts an opportunity to perform at a New Orleans club run by the unscrupulous Ace Lamont (John Miljan). Ace's girl Molly (Katherine DeMille) visits Ruby and makes it clear that she is Ace's girl. Meanwhile, Ruby becomes a hit in New Orleans, with several wealthy males interested in her, much to the chagrin of Lamont, who does not like her independence. Tiger is booked in a fight at Ace's club, and is talked into robbing a girl whom Lamont has said is blackmailing him, asking that the fighter retrieve expensive jewelry Ace claims to have given her. Tiger does not realize it is Ruby. Later, Ruby eavesdrops and sees Tiger give Lamont the stolen jewels. Ruby later turns the tables by reporting the theft to Lamont and asking him to keep her other jewels so they'll be safe. He agrees, and she uses opera glasses when he opens the safe, allowing her to see the combination. After his bout, Tiger and Ruby confront each other and it is revealed that she never cheated on him in St. Louis, and water Lamont slipped him during the fight was drugged, causing him to lose. Lamont plans to abscond with the money from his safe and burn down his club, but Ruby has already cleaned out the safe, leaving him with nothing. Ruby tells her maid (Libby Taylor) to pack their bags and summon a cab. Lamont is confronted by Molly, whom he knocks out and throws in a closet. He pours gasoline around the room and is ready to start a fire, when Tiger bursts in and punches him, inadvertently killing him. Ruby's discarded cigarette accidentally starts a fire that spreads quickly. Hearing Molly's screams, Tiger rescues her while Ruby calls the fire department. A newspaper montage

Some trade ads used the original title to promote the film

sequence reveal that Tiger is arrested, and cleared, for Lamont's death and the film ends with he and Ruby getting married.

The finished film of *Belle of the Nineties* was quite a bit different from what had been *It Ain't No Sin*. The retakes caused the budget for *Belle of the Nineties* to balloon up to $800,000, a lot of money for a movie filmed in 1933. It opens with these words flashing on the screen:

This picture approved by the Production Code Administration of the Motion Picture Producers & Distributors of America

An ominous bit of information that comes on the screen even before the studio logo, it signifies that the motion picture's creative aesthetics have now changed.

After a musical opening Ruby is about to go into her apartment with Tiger and they're stopped by an irate Kirby who is concerned about Tiger's fight that Friday and how she distracts him.

Kirby: I know she's a swell gal, but all she thinks about is having a good time.

Ruby: I don't only think about it.

Kirby insists on waiting outside the building for Tiger, and is still out there pacing once it starts pouring rain. This is the sort of comedy director McCarey presents most effectively. He shoots Kirby pacing in the rain from the vantage point of Ruby's apartment window. As he paces, we see an umbrella landing at his feet. It's a funny visual and McCarey's experience in silent comedy helps frame it effectively. When Ruby calls the cops and we see Kirby taken away, it climaxes that gag.

The set up getting Tiger to believe Ruby is cheating on him is done where one of Kirby's fighters (Warren Hymer) calls Ruby in front of him and talks like he has a date with her. Ruby, on the other line, is dismissive, thinking it is merely a fan, but Tiger only hears one side of the conversation. Mae West's acting once Tiger breaks it off with her is nicely effective, showing her toughness pushing through her sorrow. It reveals a talent for nuance in Mae's innate ability as an actress.

Once in New Orleans, Ruby is quickly confronted by Molly, after it is established that Ace Lamont thinks little of her.

Molly: So you're Ruby Carter!

Ruby: The only thing my mother ever told me, the rest I found out for myself..

Molly: I'm Ace Lamont's sweetheart!

Ruby: That's fine, he's a swell guy, you wanna hold onto him.

Molly: I guess I can do that all right.

Ruby: Then what have you got to worry about?

This establishes a dynamic that, unfortunately, isn't terribly well explored in the reworked film after the production code's edits.

After she performs a bluesy number that includes the lyric "I've got more diamonds than Uncle Sam's got marines," Ace Lamont makes a play for her:

Ace: You're the kind of woman I dreamed about always desired. I'm wild about you.

Ruby: Some of the wildest men make the best pets.

Ace: Ruby, I must have you your golden hair, your fascinating eyes, your alluring smile, and lovely arms

Ruby: Wait a minute. Is this a proposal, or are yuh takin' inventory?

Ruby sees right through his controlling nature, and but wants to keep her lucrative job. She brings up Molly and he is dismissive, so that confirms her idea about him. It is a well-played scene by both actors, exploring each character.

While Mae West presents Ruby with a wry sarcastic nature and a grounded, secure demeanor, her dialog has none of the edge found in *She Done Him Wrong* or *I'm No Angel*. Any such dialog was either removed or rewritten to appease Breen and get the film released. Even Ruby's attraction to a handsome suitor Brooks Clayburne (Johnny Mack Brown) is so tame it arouses less interest than it should, even as a conflict between him and the pursuant Ace Lamont. When Ace refuses to give Ruby a week off, she accepts it but then says, "Y'know I don't need this job. I don't need to work at all." It stands to reason that the original dialog was much more potent but rewritten due to the code.

Mae West's penchant for employing African American performers extends not only to Lilly but her insistence on Duke Ellington's band to be her musical backup. The studio balked, as Ellington was an established jazz performer who was more costly than a competent group of studio musicians. That latter might be fine for Paramount, but not for Mae West, and Ellington's band does appear. Ruby's relationship with her maid once again shows more than an employee-employer dynamic. At one point the maid states, "All my life I've been looking for a man that is big and handsome and's got plenty of money." Ruby replies, "What you've been looking for is three men."

But the real highlight regarding African American performers in this movie is a prayer meeting held by Brother Eben (George Reed) where a group of Black performers portray the congregation and sing spirituals while chanting against evil. Segregation is challenged when Ruby sings with them from the distance of her balcony, at one point the image of the congregation and her image superimposed on the screen. It is an artful visual from director McCarey. The Black community continued to support Mae West and Paramount arranged for *Belle of the Nineties* to play Black owned theaters in segregated cities. The Black owned newspaper *The California Eagle* wrote an article in June of 1934 commending *Belle of the Nineties*, stating "25 Black female extras of varying ages were used on one day, and 56 Black men were called for another."

Once *Belle of the Nineties* had been completed and was ready for release, it had to pass several censorship boards. Now that the Production Code was more seriously enforced, mentions like this one in the trade magazine *Motion Picture Daily* were popping up: "*Belle of the Nineties* has been given a clean bill of health by the Chicago and Kansas censor boards, according to Paramount. The New York board approved the picture several days ago."[30]

Despite going far over budget due to the enforced retakes, *Belle of the Nineties* still managed to turn in a healthy profit due to Mae West's massive popularity, but not as much as her previous movies.

––––––––––––––––

30   Belle Passes Boards. *Motion Picture Daily.* August 22, 1934

Judging from period reactions from theater owners, audiences did not feel it was up to the standards Mae West had already set for herself. Exhibitors complained that the altering of Mae's image affected the film and the box office:

> Expected *I'm No Angel* business and got just an average run. Spoiled in our town by the publicity it received when retakes were taken so many times.

> Mae is our best drawing card and any time she's here the S.R.O. (standing room only) sign is out. However, this picture wasn't as well liked as the others. The Legion of Decency gummed things up.

> Good picture, although the zip has been taken out of Mae's dialog. Compared with her previous pictures, it seems tame.[31]

Perhaps the most thoughtful response from an exhibitor came from theater owner Herman J. Brown of the Majestic Theater in the small town of Nampa, Idaho.

> I don't think that show business realizes yet what a wonder Mae West is. She is the greatest showman of us all. She is a genius as an actress. If I headed Paramount I would have her stick her head in on every set of every picture turned out in Hollywood. My hat is off to her. I would like to have her tell me her ideas of running a theater. I would sit quiet and listen with my large ears.[32]

Many critics, however, took the film as it was, without judging the level of edginess that might have been curtailed. Andre Sennwald of *The New York Times* stated:

> Although Mae West has graciously permitted the New York censors to make an honest woman of her in her new picture, she has not adopted the emblematic blue-

---

31 What The Picture Did For Me. *Motion Picture Herald.* November-December, 1934

32 Brown, Herman J. What The Picture Did For Me. *Motion Picture Herald.* November 17, 1934

nose. Back in the days when *Belle of the Nineties*—alias *Belle of New Orleans* and *It Ain't No Sin*—was locked in a death grip with the local censorship board, one of the major points of dissension was the shocking fade-out in which Miss West won her man without the assistance of a justice of the peace. In the new and approved version there is a wedding ceremony and Miss West is now safe for her large following to visit.It is pretty futile to strive for an air of detachment toward Miss West and her new work. A continuously hilarious burlesque of the mustache cup, celluloid collar and family entrance era of the naughty Nineties, it immediately takes its place among the best screen comedies of the year. Its incomparable star has been bolstered by a smart and funny script, an excellent physical production and a generally buoyant comic spirit. There are gags for every taste and most of them are outrageously funny according to almost any standard of humor.[33]

Meanwhile the review in the trade magazine *Photoplay* was a full-on rave, indicating the movie was among Mae's best:

You thought Mae West couldn't do it again – go and lose your bet. Also your dignity. As Ruby Carter, burlesque queen of the beef trust days, Mae is still the consummate artist of timing and delivery – and she has some knockout lines to deliver. Her costumes are something; her songs are good too. Duke Ellington's orchestra accompanies Mae's provocatively swaying hips and feathers. And the lines are so funny, without being offensive, that the outcome is a major triumph of Mae over matter.[34]

Critical reaction and the response from exhibitors and moviegoers was not as consistent in its positivity as the reviews had been for *She Done Him Wrong* and *I'm No Angel*. The chief complaint

---

33 Sennwald, Andre. Belle of the Nineties review. *The New York Times.* September 22, 1934
34 Belle of the Nineties. *Photoplay.* November, 1934

from any negative reaction was that the censor interference had taken much of the bite out of Mae West's performance. But viewing this film in the 21st Century, it remains entertaining and still showcases enough of the Mae West persona to be appealing. And its context in history is significant in that it is the first film where West had to rework her ideas due to changes in the production of movies.

Unfortunately, Mae West's battles with the censors were just beginning. Upon completing work on *Belle of the Nineties*, Mae started writing the screenplay for her next film, which she titled *Now I'm a Lady*. The production code nixed that title and it was released as *Goin' To Town*.

GOIN' TO TOWN

Directed by Alexander Hall
Screenplay by Mae West from a story by Marion Morgan and George B. Dowell
Produced by William LeBaron
Cinematography by Karl Struss
Film Editing by LeRoy Stone

Songs:
He's a Bad Man
Music by Sammy Fain
Lyrics by Irving Kahal

Now I'm a Lady
Music by Sammy Fain
Lyrics by Irving Kahal and Sam Coslow

Mon Coeur S'oeuvre A Ta Voix
from *Samson et Dalila*
Music by Camille Saint-Saëns

Love is Love
Music by Sammy Fain
Lyrics by Irving Kahal

Cast:
Mae West . . . . Cleo Borden
Paul Cavanagh . . . . Edward Carrington
Gilbert Emery . . . . Winslow
Marjorie Gateson . . . . Mrs. Crane Brittony
Tito Coral . . . . Taho
Ivan Lebedeff . . . . Ivan Valadov

Fred Kohler . . . . Buck Gonzales
Monroe Owsley . . . . Fletcher Colton
Grant Withers . . . . Young Stud
Luis Alberni . . . . Sr. Vitola
Lucio Villegas . . . . Señor Ricardo Lopez
Mona Rico . . . . Dolores Lopez
Wade Boteler . . . . Ranch foreman
Paul Harvey . . . . Donovan
Joe Frye . . . . Laughing Eagle
Vladimar Bykoff . . . . Tenor
Rafael Alcayde . . . . Sr. Alvarez
Robert Baikoff . . . . Lt. Mendoza
Eugene Borden . . . . French Captain Dupont
Adrienne D'Ambricour . . . . Annette
Virginia Hammond . . . . Miss Plunkett
Lew Kelly . . . . Michael, Colton's Gardener
Leonid Kinskey . . . . Cecil - Interior Decorator
Dewey Robinson . . . . Toby - Bartender
Morgan Wallace . . . . J. Henry Brash
George Renault . . . . Capt. Dupont
Frank Mayo . . . . Rand
Sammy Stein . . . . Cowboy
Tom London . . . . Cowboy
J.P. McGowan . . . . Cowboy
Jack Pennick . . . . Cowboy
James Pierce . . . . Cowboy
Bert Roach . . . . Cowboy
Joe Twerp . . . . Cowboy
Irving Bacon . . . . Cowboy
Jules Cowles . . . . Cowboy
Syd Saylor . . . . Cowboy
Harold Entwistle . . . . Colton's Butler
Henry Mowbray . . . . Colton's Second Butler
George Guhl . . . . Colton's Chauffeur
Carlos Villarías . . . . Cleo's Butler

Tom Monk. . . . . English Butler
O.M. Steiger. . . . . French Butler
Pauline Paquette. . . . . French Maid
 Mirra Rayo . . . . French Maid
Germaine De Neel. . . . . French Servant
Mack Gray . . . . Croupier
Gino Corrado. . . . . Bartender
Ronald R. Rondell . . . . Bookie at Bar
William Begg. . . . . Man at Bar
Jack Kennedy . . . . Man Outside Saloon
Albert Conti. . . . . Head Steward
Franco Corsaro. . . . . Italian Officer
Francis Ford . . . . Sheriff
Robert Dudley . . . . Deputy
Charles McMurphy . . . . Cop
Ted Oliver . . . . Cop
Frank McGlynn Sr. . . . . Judge
Julia Griffith. . . . . Society Dowager
Laura Treadwell . . . . Society Lady
Nell Craig. . . . . Society Lady
Andrés de Segurola . . . . Racing Association President
Stanley Andrews . . . . Engineer
Zita Baca . . . . Dancer
Dolores Duran . . . . Tango Dancer
Ramon Ros. . . . . Tango Dancer
Frank Mundin . . . . Mrs. Brittony's Jockey
Sheldon Jett . . . . Homely Polo Player
Ivor McFadden. . . . . Workman
Bert Moorhouse. . . . . Conceited Man
Manuel París . . . . Horse Bettor
Stanley Price. . . . . Attendant
Tom Ricketts . . . . Indian Seller
Cyril Ring . . . . Stage Manager
Julian Rivero. . . . . Bet Taker
Henry Roquemore . . . . The Match King

George Nardelli . . . . Party Guest
Ralph Brooks . . . . Party Guest
Dale Van Sickel . . . . Party Guest
Carl M. Leviness . . . . Nightclub Patron
Buck Russell. . . . . Nightclub Patron
Loretta Russell. . . . . Nightclub Patron
Wedgwood Nowell. . . . . Nightclub Patron
 Edmund Mortimer . . . . Nightclub Patron
James Carlisle. . . . . Nightclub Patron
Larry Steers . . . . Nightclub Patron
Bess Flowers. . . . . Nightclub Extra
Pearl Eaton. . . . . Girl

Released April 25, 1935
Paramount Pictures
Running time: 71 minutes

Mae West's charm and intelligence were enough to work around the restrictions of the Production Code and sneak in enough risqué lines in her latest movie, *Goin' To Town* to please her fans

Goin' To Town was based on a story that Paramount had purchased, and West agreed it was a good basis upon which she could write a screenplay. She wanted to make a western so she set the film in the west. She also decided she wanted to act opposite a handsome young Native American, so she made a trip to Sherman Indian School in Riverside, California where male students lined up on the football field for her to look over. Eventually that idea was jettisoned. She then wanted to borrow Cesar Romero from Universal as her leading man, but the studio would not loan him out, claiming they needed him for a project of their own (probably *Diamond Jim*).

Mae West realized her level of stardom and how her movies had saved the studio from bankruptcy, so her demands became more extreme and costlier to the studio. She insisted on having entire sequences re-shot after she watched the rushes for

Ad for Goin' To Town

that day's filming. She had her gowns redesigned after they had already been completed. She insisted on small roles for relatives who were not actors. And her tardiness kept the cast and crew waiting for as much as four hours for her arrival.

A more serious setback was when West's father Jack West died in January of 1935. She cancelled only one day of filming so she could attend his funeral, but returned to work the next day, telling reporters she didn't want the cast and crew to be out of work long.

Another distraction was the firing of Emmanuel Cohen, who had been in charge of Paramount's production since 1932. He was a strong supporter of Mae West and her films, arguing in favor of her more risqué ideas during the pre-code era, and was instrumental in decisions that allowed her to help the studio out of financial doldrums. Mae was unhappy that she lost a major studio ally. His replacement was Ernst Lubitsch, a brilliant director, but with a more exacting vision that clashed with Mae's approach.

Stories based on George Bernard Shaw's *Pygmalion,* where a crude person seeks refinement has been done by everyone from Edward G. Robinson (*Little Giant*) to The Three Stooges (*Half Wits Holiday*). Mae West's version in *Goin' To Town* has her own journey over which she explores with a streetwise introspection.

Mae West plays Cleo Borden, a saloon singer who accepts the marriage proposal of cattle rustler Buck Gonzales (Fred Kohler). An agreement is signed, but when Cleo travels to his ranch, she is told by lawyer Winslow (Gilbert Emery) that Buck has died, and that the binding marital agreement means she has inherited everything. She hires experienced people to help run the ranch, and tries to win over a handsome surveyor named Carrington (Paul Cavanagh). She follows him to Buenos Aires where she uses her charm to get ahead, but her quest is to become a "real lady" in order to be in the same league as Carrington. She finds herself at odds with society people by making a side bet on a horse race where she has a horse entered. The society woman with whom she has the wager, Mrs. Crane Brittony (Marjorie Gateson), loses the $50,000 despite attempts to cheat. Cleo is too clever to not see the planned cheat and makes her own arrangements to counter it. Cleo enters a loveless marriage to a relative of Brittony in order to gain social status. Brittony tries to frame Cleo but it backfires tragically. And Carrington returns to proclaim his love to her, having gained the title of Earl.

Director Alexander Hall stages Buck Gonzales' death effectively (he gets shot by the law while rustling cattle). He offers footage of an actual cattle drive, in the dark and in the rain, allowing for an atmospheric visual when the shooting of Gonzales occurs. In another early scene, when Cleo arrives and is told Buck is dead, a medium shot of all the ranch hands removing their hats is another effective visual.

Mae West continued to explore her innate acting ability beyond her wisecracking manner. Cleo's reaction upon hearing Buck has died is displayed with perfect nuance. She maintains her composure, but her shock and sadness is evident. When Cleo is told by

Ivan Lebedeff, Mae West, Paul Cavanagh

lawyer Winslow that she likely has inherited everything, she says, "Well, that will help pay for my feelings." Once she becomes one of the richest women in the state, she hires Winslow who agrees to "look after the cattle and the men," whereupon Cleo replies, "just the cattle, I'll take care of the men."

The next scene establishes both Carrington and Cleo's champion racehorse, but as she rides up to the stables with the ranch foreman (Wade Boteler) they have this exchange:

Foreman: We've covered quite a few miles

Cleo: I'm used to that. Except on the dance floor, it was my feet that hurt.

Cleo then rolls her eyes to convey she is talking about her derriere, and director Hall times the joke perfectly by cutting to a closeup of the smiling ranch foreman for just a few seconds, allowing the audience to get the joke without interrupting the flow of the scene. Although this exchange is brief, it shows the talent involved with the production.

Mae West, Grant Withers

When Cleo is introduced to Cactus, the race horse Buck was planning to race, it is when trainer Taho (Tito Coral) instructs jockey Laughing Eagle (Joe Frye) to take him out for a good run. Just then some cowboys doing target practice fire guns which sends the horse off running frantically, because it is "gun shy." The foreman tells Cleo that the the noise of a firecracker would allow Cactus to beat noted horserace champion Man O'War.

Cleo's attempt to get Carrington's attention fails because he considers her "crude oil." She fires a gun and knocks off his hat, but discovers that sort of playfulness that might have worked on the likes of Buck Gonzales does not work on a man of Carrington's type.

Cleo: Hmm, what do you know about me?

Carrington: Just what I see and that's quite sufficient.

Cleo: Well, you're easily satisfied.

Carrington: You possess an extraordinary sense of humor.

Cleo: Yes, and that ain't all.

However, there is a rather brilliant scene that follows when Cleo invites Carrington to her place to look over the maps of the oil wells he is surveying. First, Winslow explains to her that Carrington prefers a woman of breeding and that she is not in his social stratum. Cleo replies, "I'll make him forget he ever saw a stratum." When he arrives, it is all business. She flirts, he rejects and keeps his mind on the blueprint he has laid out on a table and is explaining.

Cleo: You're used to dames who serve pink tea and stick out their little fingers when they drink it. But I like ya anyway.

Carrington: You know, this is the first time I ever came in contact with a woman like you.

Cleo: Well, if I can help it, it won't be the last.

Carrington: You're a dangerous woman.

Cleo: Thanks. You look good to me too.

The two kiss passionately and this displays that despite the sociocultural odds that are against Cleo's manner and approach, "a man is a man," and Carrington, at least briefly, succumbs to her charm. When Winslow and the foreman walk in on them, Carrington reacts as he's been made a fool of, and leaves angrily.

When in Buenos Aires, Cleo's down-to-earth manner is looked upon by the society types as lower class, and she's clever enough to pick up on the condescension. But the men are still undeniably attracted to her. Mae West plays these scenes beautifully, as she saunters and purrs her dialog with a level of confidence that shows a superiority to the society types with only the basic rudiments of refinement provided by Winslow's casual training.

Ms. Brittony sends her boyfriend Ivan (Ivan Lebedeff) to sneak into the stable and injure Cactus, but he is caught by Taho and the

Ivan Lebedeff, Mae West, Marjorie Gateson

plot is foiled. Cleo then stations Taho near the track and instructs him to fire a gun at the right time, so a spooked Cactus runs more quickly and easily wins the race despite cheating by Brittony's jockey. This allows Cleo to win the side bet with Brittony, effectively putting the dowager in her place. She even attracts her boyfriend, who soon afterward proclaims his love for Cleo.

When Cleo and Winslow set up the marriage with Fletcher Colton (Monroe Owlsey) it comes at a time where he lost all his money from careless gambling, so he agrees to the situation as a "business proposition." He gets much needed money for allowing Cleo to use his name and stature to get into that social stratum. When society women ask questions like, "Have your ancestors ever been traced?" Cleo comes back with, "Yes, but they were too smart, they couldn't catch 'em."

Film critic and scholar Katie Carter, the author's assistant, noticed some watering down of the Mae West character:

Trade ad for Goin' To Town

I like that this film blows up the class struggle that Mae West made a part of her previous movies and sort of makes it the main conflict, with her pushing back against all of the society people who literally say she, a woman perceived as low class and poor breeding who suddenly comes into money, doesn't belong with them. West still gets a lot of great bawdy one-liners in under the code, but it seems pretty clear that the code also really affected the outcome of the conflict, and I didn't love the final act, which seems to endorse changing your ways to fit in with the upper class as opposed to carving out your own way in the world, which is how West's characters had always operated before.

One of the highlights of *Goin' To Town* is when Cleo arranges to perform in an opera to exhibit refinement in her art, which is usually blues numbers. This scene shows another level of Mae West's talent, and she worked with a voice teacher carefully so that her presentation of the aria from *Samson and Delilah* was effective. It was as much Mae West exhibiting another level as it was for the character of Cleo.

Goin' To Town had a successful premiere was ready for release in early April, but Paramount withheld it when a Milwaukee WPA worker was going through old files and discovered a 1911 marriage certificate between Mae West and a man named Frank Wallace. Newspapers were contacted and soon reporters were seeking out info on Wallace, finally finding him. Mae West denied the marriage, Wallace admitted to it, but stated they had divorced and he had been married to another since 1916. When no divorce papers could be found, his second wife left him. Seeing an opportunity, Wallace began billing himself as Mr. Mae West in his stage appearances. Then, to further complicate matters, Frank Wallace sued Mae, claiming that her denials of their marriage had caused him to be considered a fraud and had restricted his livelihood.

While this now seems absurd, at the time it was quite serious. This was a time when the marriages of movie stars were often kept quiet so as not to affect their image. Having Mae West married would especially cause a problem with her screen persona as being free of domesticity. Attempts were made to find a signature on the existing document to see if it matched up with Mae West's. But an article in the *Post-Crescent* out of Appleton, Wisconsin stated:

They didnt have to sign marriage licenses in Milwaukee in 1911. So, the mystery of a Mae West marrying here 24 years ago and giving license data which checks in some details with the known facts about the state and screen actress, remains unsolved. Plans were made to compare the signature of the well known Mae West of 1935 with that appearing on the license taken by one Mae West and Frank Wallace here in 1911. But it was found that the county clerk had written all of the names on the license. Nowhere was there a Westian signature.[35]

However, despite all of this negative publicity, *Goin' To Town* did not suffer at the box office. Audiences still liked Mae West and were eager to see how much she got past the restrictive censors. While Joseph Breen approved the film when screened prior to release, the religious groups once again swooped in and complained that Breen was being too lenient with this controversial star's films. But that just added to the moviegoers' interest. The spring release date for this movie seemed to provide some pretty convenient marketing points—a lot of old ads claim "Mae is coming" and "Get ready for Mae Day."

One of the strongest promotional pieces was credited to Susan Hartwell in *Silver Screen*, but it was clearly marked as an advertisement. It stated:

> Just a brief two years ago Mae West changed the feminine contours of the world when she swpet across the cinematic heavens in *She Done Him Wrong*. Now the versatile Mae is about to do the same thing again, to the delight of the fashion designers and her legions of feminine and masculine fans. But this time she's offering a streamlined silhouette instead of the full-rounded curves of two seasons ago. And the story and background of *Goin To Town* offers just as much contrast to her previous vehicles as the Mae West of 1935 does to the Mae West of 1933. The fashionable spots of smart, present-

---

35 No Signature. *Post-Crescent.* April 22, 1935.

day society – Long Island, New York and Buenos Aries, Argentina, for instance – replace the Bowery of the Nineties and the gay spots of New Orleans a generation ago as the setting for the action of her new picture. Even her leading men have undergone a radical change. Gone are the prizefighters and gamblers of an older era; instead honors are shared by Paul Cavanagh, the suavest of suave Anglo-American actors and Ivan Lebedeff, ace of the heel-clicking, hand-kissing heart-smashers. So watch out for the New Mae West. She is going to set a new standard in entertainment, in wise-cracks, in fashions, and in the feminine form divine when Paramount's *Goin' To Town* reaches the screens of the world.[36]

This promotional piece was an obvious attempt at Paramount to sell the watered-down changes to their risqué performer as a positive progression, especially touting the fact that her film's setting is contemporary times. The studio was concerned by *Belle of the Nineties* grossing a lower amount at the box office than its predecessors. Paramount realized they had to adhere to the Production Code's parameters, but didn't want to sacrifice the box office numbers of their star who was most known for her risqué material.

Reviews were generally good, with *Film Daily* calling it "Another load of wisecracks in a nicely sustained story,"[37] and an exhibitor from a small town in Michigan wrote to the trades: "Biggest Wednesday gross in 1935. If it brings in the cash, and pleases the majority what more can we ask?"[38] Some creative publicity stunts were also happening:

Through a tie-up with police department, T. H. Read, Paramount in Atlanta, Ga., placed "Drive carefully when you're Goin' To Town" cards on all posts as a plug. Letters were mailed to leading merchants who cooperated by

---

36   Hartwell, Susan. The New Streamlined Mae West. *Silver Screen.* May, 1935

37   Goin to Town review. *Film Daily.* April 25, 1935

38   What the Picture Did for Me. *Motion Picture Herald.* October 5, 1935

using the title in their ads, and the bus company carried banners. The leading sausage company tied in by offering tickets to salesmen selling the largest number of weenies during their "Goin' To Town with Sausages" week. Tickets were also awarded in a radio contest covering typical southern recipes.[39]

Goin' To Town was yet another box office success, but due to its overblown budget, the net profit for the studio was the least of Mae's films thus far. West was feeling a bit less welcome at the studio with the shakeups at the top, including the aforementioned firing of Cohen, and the Paramount workers were becoming a bit more chagrined by West's diva-like behavior. But this did not stop anyone from preparing for Mae West's next feature, *Klondike Annie.*

---

39 Read Placards Town with Goin' To Town Cards. *Motion Picture Herald.* July 20, 1935

KLONDIKE ANNIE

Directed by Raoul Walsh
Screenplay by Mae West, based on her play, from a story by Marion Morgan and George B. Dowell with contributions from Frank Mitchell Dazey, Bert Hanlon, Boris Petroff
Produced by William LeBaron
Cinematography by George T. Clemens
Film Editing by Stuart Heisler

Songs:
My Medicine Man
Written by Sam Coslow

Cheer Up, Little Sister
Written by Gene Austin

It's Better to Give Than to Receive
Written by Gene Austin

I'm an Occidental Woman in an Oriental Mood for Love
Written by Gene Austin

Mister Deep Blue Sea
Written by Gene Austin & James P. Johnson

Little Bar Butterfly
Written by Gene Austin

Cast:
Mae West . . . . Rose Carlton
Victor McLaglen . . . . Bull Brackett
Phillip Reed . . . . Insp. Jack Forrest

Helen Jerome Eddy . . . . Sister Annie Alden
Harry Beresford . . . . Brother Bowser
Harold Huber. . . . . Chan Lo
Lucile Gleason . . . . Big Tess
Conway Tearle . . . . Vance Palmer
Esther Howard. . . . . Fanny Radler
Soo Yong . . . . Fah Wong, Rose's Maid
John Rogers . . . . Buddie
Ted Oliver . . . . Grigsby
Lawrence Grant . . . . Sir Gilbert
Gene Austin. . . . . Organist
Vladimar Bykoff. . . . . Marinoff
Maidel Turner . . . . Lydia Bowley
Huntley Gordon. . . . . Clinton Reynolds
Russ Hall . . . . Candy
Otto Heimel. . . . . Cocoa
Guy D'Ennery . . . . Alverados
Tetsu Komai. . . . . Lan Fang
Philip Ahn . . . . Wing
Mrs. Wong Wing. . . . . Ah Toy
Wong Chung . . . . Tong Man
Paul Fung . . . . Tong Man
Mrs. Chan Lee . . . . Blind Woman
Marcel Ventura. . . . . Frenchman
Jack Mulhall. . . . . Officer
Jack Daley. . . . . Second Mate
Jack Wallace . . . . Third Mate
John Lester Johnson. . . . . Sailor
Ed Brady . . . . Sailor
John Lester Johnson. . . . . Sailor
Chester Gan. . . . . Ship's Cook
George Walsh. . . . . Quartermaster
James Burke . . . . Bartender
Homer Dickenson . . . . Dress Man
Jackson Snyder . . . . Little Boy

Polly Bailey.	Mission Woman
William Bailey	Mission Man
Nella Walker	Missionary
D'Arcy Corrigan	Missionary
Nell Craig.	Missionary
Art Foster.	Missionary
Eddie Allen	Miner
Richard Allen.	Miner
Howard Lang.	Miner
Kathrin Clare Ward	Miner's Wife
George MacQuarrie.	Port Officer
Carl Harbaugh.	Port Officer
George Burton	Port Official
Frank Baker	Port Official
Marie Wells	Dance Hall Girl
Kathleen Key	Dance Hall Girl
Ilean Hume	Dance Hall Girl
Gladys Gale	Dance Hall Girl
Elsie Dempsey	Dance Hall Girl
Edna Bennett.	Dance Hall Girl
Pearl Eaton.	Dance Hall Girl

Released February 21, 1936
Paramount Pictures
78 minutes

With *Klondike Annie*, Mae West had her biggest and most disruptive battles with the censors. While the Breen office was initially satisfied, the various other groups made a lot of noise condemning the film's content and complained that the censorship board, despite greater adherence to the production code, had fallen short in their reaction to this film.

Before *Klondike Annie* could begin production, Mae West had to deal with a serious matter in her offscreen life. Receiving anonymous phone calls threatening to throw acid in her face, or murder

Mae West continued to stir up controversy

her, West was told to drop $1000 in cash in a designated area to avoid disfigurement or death. When this was arranged under police surveillance, a 38-year-old Greek studio busboy, George Janios, went to retrieve the package and was arrested. Janios, who spoke little English, claimed he was a random passerby who happened upon the package. The district attorney felt that perhaps Janios was a go-between for the actual extortionists. When the FBI took over the case, Janios was released from custody. When the actual culprit was captured, Mae was back at the studio, ready to work, the very next day. She quipped to the press, "Nothing to it, I always get my man."

Klondike Annie was based on Mae West's 1921 play *Frisco Kate*, as well as a story by a Marion Morgan and George Brendan Dowell. Combining the two concepts, Mae created a screenplay originally titled *Klondike Lou* but changed during production. Filming was

Ad for Klondike Annie

off to a bit of a rocky start when Mae protested not getting Karl Struss as her cinematographer. Struss was active on other projects, so George T. Clemens was hired. Clemens would later be known as cinematographer for the *Twilight Zone* TV series. But when hired for *Klondike Annie*, he was a very young unknown whose only other project had been a short film for Paramount about ballet. West was displeased with his lack of experience.

One thing that did please West was the hiring of director Raoul Walsh. Walsh was very open to West's creative suggestions and collaborated closely with her. In his autobiography, he recalled that West was chastised by production head Ernst Lubitsch for arriving late to production, so West purposely arrived late each day just to upset the producer. Despite these disruptive situations, *Klondike Annie* did get made with a budget of $1,000,000.

Mae West plays Rose Carlton, an entertainer known as The Frisco Doll, who is the charge of Chan Lo (Harold Huber). When she kills him in self-defense, she flees to Alaska on a steamer ship where she meets Sister Annie Alden (Helen Jerome Eddy). When Sister Annie dies before reaching her destination, Rose takes her name and identity and carries on with the nun's quest to help a mission in Nome that has fallen on hard financial times. Rose is inspired by Annie's teachings so she tries to maintain the promise to rescue the troubled mission, by combining her newfound respect for religion with her cunning and savvy. In the meantime, she is romanced by rugged Bull Bracket (Victor McLaglen) and a curious lawman (Phillip Reed). In the end she returns to San Francisco with Bull, intent on clearing her name and proving she acted in self-defense.

Mae West plays Rose Carlton as tough, even when playing against Chan Lo, who is supposedly in charge of her. The film finds her at a point where she has become weary of her limitations:

> Rose: Why do you keep me from having friends of my own race?

> Chan Lo: Because it is written there are two perfectly good men. One dead, the other unborn.

> Rose: Which one are you?

This situation continues to present Rose's defiance when she is with her maid Fah Wong, who expresses concern:

> Fah Wong: I am afraid for you. Chan Lo would kill you before he lets you go.

> Rose: I know but I gotta take that chance. I'm tired of being a prisoner

Mae does a nice job of presenting Rose's conflict. While she doesn't appear to feel indebted to Chan Lo, she is still pondering

Mae West and Soo Yong

a sense of loyalty, an understanding of the dangers, but, mostly, her overriding need for freedom. This freedom involves her interest in the gold rush currently happening in Alaska and how the money she could gain would ensure her independence.

Rose's first meeting with Bull is when she goes aboard his boat with Fah Wong to escape. His tough, violent demeanor with his crew is briefly shown, but when he sees Rose that demeanor changes. Rose is unfazed, even when crew members peek in her bedroom window, telling Fah Wong, "it ain't the first time." Victor McLaglen had carved out a niche playing rugged characters, all the way back to the silent era. Just the previous year he had scored big with his Oscar winning performance in John Ford's

The Informer. Here his ruggedness is tamed by West's character, and the two offer a distinct chemistry on screen. Rose's murder of Chan Lo is not referenced until after she is established on Bull's ship and he discovers the information. He is angered by not having been informed, but by that time he has fallen for her, stating, "I couldn't give you up if you killed a million guys." Rose responds to his affection.

The development of Rose and Sister Annie's friendship is nicely done, with the nun showing understanding and patience, while Rose is alternately amused and bemused by the newcomer to the ship.

Sister Annie: Too many girls follow the line of least resistance

Rose: Yeah, but a good line is hard to resist.

The Sister is honest about her misgivings toward Rose's lifestyle, and despite her bravado, Rose responds with some respect for the Sister. She accepts the nun's lending to her a book of devotions.

Some of Mae West's finest acting occurs when Sister Annie dies. She exhibits real sorrow, bringing down her defiant attitude. This changes fairly quickly as a police inspector approaches the ship on a boat. It is then that Rose has the idea to trade places with Sister Annie. A scene was shot where she changes clothes with the dead woman and applies makeup to her face, switching identities with her to avoid prosecution. That specific scene was removed before release. However, they do include a shot of Rose leaving the room to meet the cops in nun's garb, introducing herself as Sister Annie, and Bull indicating Rose had died at sea.

The film then alternates between Rose's romance with Bull, situation with the curious Inspector Forrest, and her attempting to please the people of Nome who have been hoping her presence will help tame the disruptive city. Rose's attempt to avoid using street slang is an amusing touch, with Bull stating, "another day of this and you'll end up in the nuthouse." However, she finally succumbs and presents herself as Sister Annie with all of Rose's street savvy:

Trade ad for Klondike Annie

Now I'll tell ya - you people have been on the wrong
track, and I'm gonna steer you right You'll never get
anywhere because you don't know how to wrassle the
devil. Tying a knot in his tail won't throw 'im on his back;
you've gotta grab 'im by his horns - you've gotta know
him, know his tricks. I know 'em, and how I know 'em!

Why, I can make him say uncle - that is, if he's got an
uncle.

One of director Raoul Walsh's strongest films of only a few years
earlier was *The Bowery* (1933), so his attention to detail showing
the ruggedness of 1890s saloon life is colorful and authentic. And
Rose, as Annie, confronting the bar owners in their own language
is effective in getting things done. There is an amusing scene with
Bull grabbing people and tossing them into the Settlement House
where Rose and her new group are holding a religious revival
meeting. While the minister gets nowhere with this rowdy crowd,
Rose is most effective conveying a newfound religious spirit to all
of them.

Mae West continued to expand upon her screen persona, working to stay within the Production Code parameters while exploring how she could bring her stage characters to the screen. The
character of Rose is one of her deepest and most fulfilling, her
charisma managing to bring estranged couples together, keep men
from irresponsible drinking, and other accomplishments the pious
wish to accomplish but cannot. The minister states, "We have
people here tonight we didn't dare to hope for and we owe it all to
you." She even gets a couple of tough mug friends to do the col-
lections, making sure that the coffers are filled.

While the Inspector character has a significance to the narrative
-- Rose on the run in disguise would require a lawman as part of
the plot – the unlikely romance between him and Rose, and the
conflict between him and Bull, seems tangential. His sudden falling for Rose and ready to turn his back on being a lawman doesn't
ring completely true.. This is not the fault of actor Phillip Reed,
who played second leads quite effectively in a career that spanned
over 30 years, in movies starring everyone from James Cagney to
Elvis Presley. He also did a great deal of TV work.

Mae West wanted Chinese people to play the Chinese characters and, for the most part, this was done, but American actor
Harold Huber played the Chan Lo role. Huber, who specialized
in playing gangsters and tough guys in films like *The Thin Man*

Phillip Reed and Mae West

(1934) and *G Men* (1935), was primarily hired because Paramount realized having a white actress being "kept" by a Chinese man, where a sexual relationship is implied at all, was going to be difficult enough to get past the censors. Casting a Chinese actor would only add to the controversy. Mae West argued that young newcomer Phillip Ahn, being an American of Chinese descent, should take the role, but he is relegated to a mere bit part.

The opening night of *Klondike Annie* in New York City made a big splash, according to Phil M. Daly's column Around the Rialto:

> The New York Paramount Theater celebrated another
> Mae West Day with the opening of *Klondike Annie*.
> Rivaling the Worlds Series, the box office line at the
> Times Square house started to form at 8am. The number
> one man in line was an elderly gentleman from New-
> ark who had been a Mae West fan for many years. At

8am the queue stretched from the Paramount box-office around the corner on 43rd Street to the New York Times offices. A packed house throughout the morning necessitated an increase in the operating personnel of the theater, requiring 33 additional ushers, 11 doormen, 4 porters, and 4 maids to take care of the crowd. By 10am the house was full. By 11am there was a complete fill in the lobby. At noon 2000 formed a new street line.[40]

Klondike Annie was barely in theaters a month before a huge censorship campaign came crashing down on it, mostly due to a reaction by the powerful William Randolph Hearst. A newspaper magnate, Hearst condemned the film in a column that was syndicated in all of his many newspapers. Along with panning the film as lewd, it exhibited a bigoted reaction to the Chinese characters in the film and their connection to the title character:

Are we again to have placed before us in the guise of entertainment motion pictures that exalt disreputable living and glorify vice? The question naturally arises after viewing the Mae West picture, *Klondike Annie*. It is an immoral and indecent film. What were Will Hays and his censorship organization doing when this deliberate catering to a lewd element came forth? It is their specific duty, their job, to make sure that only motion pictures of a wholesome, healthy character are produced. Censors in some States may cut a few of the worst scenes, but they cannot cleanse it. For the most part, cleaner and better pictures have been brought forth by the producers in the past year than ever before. The public's response has evidenced beyond doubt its appreciation and support of that trend, but one indecent film may tear down much of the good will that has been built. Therefore, it is astounding that Paramount should have had the stupidity to produce and distribute such a picture, when it has been demonstrated to what a degree the screen has benefited by the

40   Daly, Phil M. Along The Rialto. *The Film Daily.* March 12, 1936

clean pictures produced since the public uprising against screen filth. Decent people will protest against this Mae West picture, against the depiction on the screen, in any form, of vulgarity and lust, and against showing a white woman in the role, even inferred, of consort to a Chinese vice lord. It is to be hoped that the churches of the country are awake to the necessity of boycotting such a picture as *Klondike Annie* and denouncing its producers. This offering would apparently indicate that some screen producers are not influenced by any moral considerations, but only by fear of public indignation. Therefore, the public should bring such influence to bear by showing through non-patronage of such productions that pandering to the lewd elements of the community is not profitable.[41]

Despite being accepted by the Production Code, *Klondike Annie* aroused the ire of the Catholic Legion of Decency for the concept of a chorus girl hiding out as a nun, and utilizing her own streetwise manner to the character she has assumed. Hearst then used that as a starting point to begin his campaign against the film, the real reason, as claimed by some editorials in the trade magazines, was because Mae West refused to appear on one of his radio shows.

In an article entitled Exhibitor Answers Hearst Attack, theater owner J.L. Schanberger, manager of Keith's Theater in Baltimore stated:

> There is no record of any of the state or local censorship boards ordering deletions in *Klondike Annie* or refusing it an exhibition permit. State boards are in New York, Pennsylvania, Ohio, Kansas, Florida, Maryland, Massachusetts, and Virginia. The picture has already played in every one of those states. No opposition was heard from any of the foregoing towns until Mr. Hearst undertook his attack.[42]

---

41   Stop Lewd Films. *San Francisco Examiner.* February 29, 1936

42   Exhibitor Answers Hearst Attack. *Motion Picture Herald.* March 7, 1936.

Prizefighter James J. Braddock (left) visited the set and posed with Mae West and director Raoul Walsh

Reviews for the film were consistently negative in all of the many Hearst newspapers, but in those papers that Hearst did not control, the reaction was different. *The New York Times* even addressed the controversy, stating:

> Mae West's *Klondike Annie* really does not merit the
> agitation it has caused. Neither as healthily rowdy nor as
> vulgarly suggestive as many of her earlier pictures. It is, of
> course, highly ironic that the more she attempts to please
> the censors the more she displeases them.[43]

Meanwhile, *Variety* reported that Hearst's attack on the movie, and his refusing to allow theaters to advertise it did not amount to much impact. The headline of their story was "Hearst Papers Steam Up on West Pic So Far a Boon to the B.O."

> The Hearst-West tilt is arousing concern within Para-
> mount, but in all probability helping the picture at the
> box office, is regarded by the company as some kind of a
> personal fight someone is waging with Miss West. The
> company discussed the matter at length at last week's
> board meeting but is taking no action. Instead it is mov-
> ing up playdates in some spots in the thought that the
> current publicity, whether to be regarded good or bad, is a
> box office stimulant.[44]

Tired of the battles with both the censors and production head Ernst Lubitsch, and seeing her creative control more limited, Mae West signed with independent producer Emmauel Cohen, who had once worked at Paramount and was always supportive of her creativity. After forming his own production company, Cohen had taken on Paramount as a partner and was releasing his films through them, so West still had the support of the same major studio. However, her next film, *Go West Young Man*, once again resulted in another battle with the censors.

---

43 Klondike Annie Review. *The New York Times*. March 12, 1936.
44 Hearst-Block Papers Steam Up on West Pic So Far a Boon to the B.O.

GO WEST YOUNG MAN

Directed by Henry Hathaway
Screenplay by Mae West from the play by Lawrence Riley
Produced by Emanuel Cohen
Cinematography by Karl Struss
Film Editing by Ray Curtiss

Songs:
On A Typical Tropical Night
Written by Arthur Johnston
Lyrics by Johnny Burke

I Was Saying To The Moon
Written by Arthur Johnston
Lyrics by Johnny Burke

Cast:
Mae West . . . . Mavis Arden
Warren William . . . . Morgan
Randolph Scott . . . . Bud Norton
Alice Brady . . . . Mrs. Struthers
Elizabeth Patterson . . . . Aunt Kate Barnaby
Lyle Talbot . . . . Francis X. Harrigan
Isabel Jewell . . . . Gladys
Margaret Perry . . . . Joyce Struthers
Etienne Girardot . . . . Prof. Herbert Rigby
Maynard Holmes . . . . Clyde
John Indrisano . . . . Chauffeur
Alyce Ardell . . . . Jeanette
Nick Stewart . . . . Nicodemus
Charles Irwin . . . . Master of Ceremonies
Walter Walker . . . . Kelton

Harold Minjir. . . . . Cummings
Russ Powell . . . . Andy
Si Jenks. Bumpkin
Hugh Chapman . . . . Townfolk Boy
Elaine Koehler . . . . Little Girl
Jack La Rue . . . . Rico in Drifting Lady
G.P. Huntley . . . . Philip in Drifting Lady
Robert Baikoff . . . . Officer in Drifting Lady
Raquel Torres . . . . Rico's Girlfriend in
                                             Drifting Lady
Xavier Cugat . . . . Orchestra Leader
Dick Elliott . . . . Union News Service
Reporter
Cyril Ring . . . . Reporter
Lester Dorr . . . . Reporter
Eddie Fetherston . . . . Reporter
Eddie Dunn . . . . Security Guard at Theatre
Tom Hanlon. . . . . Police Radio Dispatcher
Jack Perrin . . . . Cop
Lee Shumway. . . . . Cop

Released November 18, 1936
Emmanuel Cohen Productions
Major Pictures Corporation
Paramount Pictures
80 minutes

The way Mae West got out of her Paramount contract was due
to the studio not releasing *Klondike Annie* until after the new
year. West's contract specifically called for two released pictures
per year, and when *Goin' To Town* became her only 1935 release,
she considered her contract violated. Paramount argued that it
was West's fault for not having a movie ready for release in time.
Angered by the studio's response (she calculated that she had made
nearly $15 million for the studio) Mae put on a black wig and, in

Ad for Go West Young Man

disguise, went to Chicago to meet Emmanuel Cohen. In 1936 the movie industry was strong, and many independent producers started their own studios, often securing distribution deals with the majors. After negotiating with Cohen, Mae West returned to the studio and found that Lubitsch had returned to being a director and one of West's strongest supporters, William LeBaron, was promoted to production head.

Responding to the change in leadership at Paramount, West's manager James Timony told the press that Lubitsch thought "in his Hitler-like manner he could push Mae West around." When asked for a response, Lubitsch stated, "Push her around? She's much too heavy!" Mae had gained weight since entering films and was proud of her more ample figure. Articles, however, said such disparaging things as "Plumpness is an insidious thing, it sneaks up on you and becomes just plain fat."

After signing with independent producer Emmanuel Cohen, Mae West moved all of her belongings from her Paramount dressing room and had them brought to Cohen's studio, Major Moving Pictures. Supervising the movers carefully, Mae followed them in her limousine and made sure her setup at the new studio was exactly as she wanted. With LeBaron as production chief, Cohen had no trouble arranging a distribution deal with Paramount. So, despite her filming for an independent producer, Paramount "supplied her with their directors, cameramen, cast, and crew, as well as handling her publicity and putting their name all over her films."

West and Cohen were interested in filming Lawrence Riley's play *Personal Appearance,* about a haughty star who gets stuck in the sticks when her car breaks down, and ends up meeting a handsome, affable young man. Both Cohen and West liked the film's satirical attack on moviemaking and publicity, both of them now having struck out on their own after being treated unfairly at the same big studio. They had a battle on their hands with the Breen Office right away. Attempts to film the play were thwarted because the censors felt it presented a negative image of the industry. Cohen offered a series of script revisions and cuts from the play before the Breen Office finally approved it for filming.

Mae West plays Mavis Arden, a temperamental movie star who is believed by her fans to be charming and reserved. While on tour promoting her latest movie, Mavis and her manager Morgan (Warren William) are stranded in a small town when their car breaks down en route to meet politician Francis Harrigan (Lyle Talbot), an old flame, at a campaign stop in Harrisburg, PA.

Mae West

While their car is being repaired, they stay at a rooming house owned by Mrs. Struthers (Alice Brady) along with her daughter Joyce (Margaret Perry) and her Aunt Kate (Elizabeth Patterson). While there, Mavis meets Bud (Randolph Scott), a handsome, affable mechanic who is Joyce's beau. Mavis easily seduces Bud, much to both Joyce's and Morgan's chagrin. When Harrigan cannot reach Mavis by telephone, he overhears something about a kidnapping and believes Mavis has been kidnapped. Meanwhile,

Morgan shows Mavis baby clothing that Aunt Kate is knitting and implies that Joyce is pregnant with Bud's child. Not wanting to come between that, Mavis tells Bud it's over. Later, Aunt Kate reveals that she is knitting something for another relative so Mavis punches Morgan. Harrigan then arrives with the police, ready to arrest Morgan for kidnapping Mavis but she stops them. Morgan confesses his love for Mavis and they drive away with a police escort.

Go West Young Man is a bit offbeat for Mae West in that she plays a haughty, temperamental star rather than a flirty supporter of the working class. It was Mae wanting to satirize Hollywood and its stars that drew her and Cohen to Lawrence Riley's play, and she turns in a very good performance playing a character outside of her established persona. Randolph Scott seems a bit stiff and dull here, especially when compared to the westerns he had already made up to this time. The casting of Scott in this role might have had something to do with this film's director, Henry Hathaway, who had helmed many of the actor's earlier westerns. The supporting cast is generally appealing, some of the standouts including Warren William, the chief cad of 1930s cinema, Elizabeth Patterson, and Isabel Jewell as an emotional, star struck worker at the boarding house. Among the film's highlights include Patterson going off alone and trying to mimic Mavis' distinctive walk (which is, of course, Mae West's walk). Patterson would later be best known as the elderly Mrs Trumbull on TV's *I Love Lucy*.

Mae West continued to battle with the censors, despite being given greater creative freedom in this independent production. She insisted on the casting of Black comedian Nick Stewart as a slow-talking mechanic and wanted other Black actors in supporting roles. The censors limited segregation during these times, so only Stewart appears. Mae intended to cast a Black woman as a sharp, witty counterpart to Nick's slow talking character, but the censors refused. West knew that Stewart had perfected that comic stereotype for movies and wanted a balance. Stewart would continue to play this same character well into the TV age, although he

Mae West, Randolph Scott

was best known as a dancer and dance instructor, who ran his own studio. Nick and his wife Edna later owned the Ebony Theater in Los Angeles where many Black performers got their start.

Los Angeles Times reporter caught up with Mae West for an interview to discuss her recent career situation, censorship, and even her admiration for Charlie Chaplin's work:

> "It just breaks my heart when the censors take out my best cracks," sighed the sensational Mae West, as she sat in her smart limousine, draped in a priceless silver fox. "So in writing the screen play and dialogue for *Go West, Young Man* I had to be pretty cagey. I guess I got by with some pretty good ones at that. It still rankles the way they

edited *Klondike Annie*." Mae, looking the quintessence of innocence, told how she had one character saying, "It's hard for a pretty woman to be good, I guess," with Mae replying, "Yes, give a man a free hand and he'll put it all over you." "You know my audience wants me bad. I'm always sensational. In ten years, I've never' had a flop. My plays ran in New York over a couple of years each. And all my pictures have grossed millions. Audiences don't want me settled and domestic. But there's certainly a raft of husbands trying to claim me in real life. I go to a picture once in a while, but mostly I'm hunting up story material. I nearly butted into Charlie Chaplin's affairs recently. Could hardly resist telling him to snatch up *Three Men on a Horse* and do the little guy that does all the figuring himself. That's the worst of it, I'm always seeing good stuff for other people. I guess Charlie is my favorite actor, anyway." After ten years of sensational success as author, director, actress, with such a definitely exceptional line of her own, she is finding it a bit exacting to maintain the pace and standard. She talks to convince herself most of the time. That word "'sensational'" haunts her. The dratted thing has to be lived up to forever now. And she must forever be ebulliently, triumphantly "bad." Naughty wisecracks must drip from her lips.[45]

Go West Young Man is the first movie shot on Cohen's new lot, which had once been General Service Studios. The film has some amusing moments, but overall, it does not have the same zip as Mae West's previous films. It is a bit slow and draggy in spots, but is sustained by a top cast turning in commendable performances. Perhaps if it contained more of the lines and characters that were cut in pre-production to please the censors, it might have resulted in a better film.

---

45 Whittaker, Alma. Censors Break Heart Says Mae West. *The Los Angeles Times*. November 22, 1936

*"Whichever one o' yew boys cuts th' most wood today kin
go see the Mae West picher tonight."*

Cartoonists helped promote Go West Young Man

There were some interesting publicity ideas to promote *Go West Young Man*. One of them was the hiring of several cartoonists to offer one-panel comics to the trades, promoting the film. A distributor in Harrisburg, PA inserted the line "What Did Horace Greeley Say?" in all the daily newspapers for two weeks, and at the end it changed to "Horace Greeley said Go West Young Man." The film was then presented in a midnight sneak preview the Wednesday night before Thanksgiving.

Critics generally liked *Go West Young Man*, although *Variety* admitted that West's screen character was "no longer is quite the novelty it once was." Audiences responded favorably for the most part, but some exhibitors complained of walkouts with one stating that it was "Mae West's worst picture and hopefully her last."

While this was not West's last picture, she was becoming weary of the movies. While she was enjoying a bit more creative freedom on this independent production, she continued to battle the censors in order to get her films produced and released. Her next film, *Every Day's a Holiday* would turn out to be her cleanest picture – and her dullest.

Every Day's a Holiday

Directed by A. Edward Sutherland
Screenplay by Mae West
Produced by Emmanuel Cohen
Cinematography by Karl Struss
Film Editing by Ray Curtiss

Songs:
Fifi
Written by Sam Coslow

Little Butterfly
Written by Sam Coslow

Every Day's a Holiday
Written by Sam Coslow and Barry Trivers

Jubilee
Written by Hoagy Carmichael & Stanley Adams

Cast:
Mae West . . . . Peaches O'Day
Edmund Lowe . . . . Police Captain Jim McCarey
Charles Butterworth . . . . Larmadou Graves
Charles Winninger . . . . Van Reighle Van Pelter
Van Doon
Walter Catlett . . . . Nifty Bailey
Lloyd Nolan . . . . John Quade
Louis Armstrong . . . . Jubilee Band Leader
George Rector . . . . George Rector
Herman Bing . . . . Fritz Krausmeyer
Roger Imhof . . . . Trigger Mike

Chester Conklin. . . . . Cabby
Lucien Prival . . . . Danny the Dip
Adrian Morris . . . . Henchman
Francis McDonald . . . . Henchman
John Indrisano . . . . Henchman
Irving Bacon. . . . . Quartet Member
Allen Rogers. . . . . Quartet Member
John 'Skins' Miller . . . . Quartet Member
Otto Fries. . . . . Quartet Member
James C. Morton . . . . Bartender
Dick Elliott . . . . Bar Patron
Johnny Arthur . . . . Theatre Cashier
Edgar Dearing . . . . Cop
Maude Eburne. . . . . Dowager at Rector's
Weldon Heyburn . . . . Guest at Party
Ferdinand Munier . . . . Guest at Party
Herbert Rawlinson. . . . . Guest at Party
DeForest Covan . . . . Dancer

Released December 31, 1936
Emmanuel Cohen Productions
Major Pictures Corporation
Paramount Pictures
79 minutes

Mae West approached producer Emmanuel Cohen with the idea of playing Catherine the Great in her next movie. Believing she was now to enjoy greater creative control over her projects, she felt the producer would accept the idea and she could get to work on a script. Unfortunately for Mae, this did not happen. Cohen not only rejected her idea to play the Russian empress, he had another one in mind for West, and was already having sets built and costumes designed. Cohen's reasoning was due to Marlene Dietrich playing Catherine in *The Scarlet Empress* (1934). That film had a bloated budget of $900,000, and failed to make its costs

Mae West

back. Considered a commercial and critical failure, Cohen was not interested in his studio visiting the same story.

Believing a Gay Nineties story would best suit Mae West, he presented her with a screenplay, which she rejected, stubbornly insisting on playing Catherine the Great. Cohen worked hard to convince Mae to film his idea. He hired her favorite cinematographer, Karl Struss, had gowns designed by Italian designer Elsa Schiaparelli, whose Paris shop was noted for eccentric, surreal creations. Mae finally agreed to at least hear the songs composed for the film, so this was arranged. The song Mae liked best was the one Cohen liked least, but she was so inspired by Sam Coslow's "Fifi" that she decided to create a script based on the character in that song. Mae would play a blonde nightclub entertainer who puts on a black wig and passes as a French singer. The title would be *Every Day's a Holiday.*

Cohen brought the first draft of Mae's script to Joseph Breen, indicating that West had worked hard to create a screenplay that was clean enough for the censors' approval. Perhaps due to his chagrin at his original idea being jettisoned, Cohen worked closely with Breen. One of Mae West's strongest supporters was now working with the censors, asking for more scenes cut and further restrictions on Mae's latest script. With no support from her producer, Mae could not fight the censors, so every bit of clever double-meaning dialog was jettisoned.

Mae did win one significant battle. She insisted on having jazz musician Louis Armtrong in the movie. Armstrong would later recall: "Miss West went to the head of Paramount and told them they'd better hire me or else." West was good friends with Armstrong and thought nothing of having lunch with him in her dressing room. Armstrong recalled, "that was unheard of at the time – for a white star to mix with any Black." [46] Armstrong was allowed final approval of the film's music.

Despite *Every Day's a Holiday* being the cleanest script Mae West had written, her promoting the movie was another thing entirely, and showed how the public was now reacting to her. Mae appeared on the very popular radio show hosted by Edgar Bergen and Charlie McCarthy, and an Adam and Eve sketch she performed was considered to be in very bad taste for radio. The next day, newspapers cried for censorship for the airwaves:

> If you listened to Edgar Bergen and Charlie McCarthy
> Sunday you heard Mae West in that skit based on Adam
> and Eve in the Garden of Eden. It was in very bad taste,
> especially as the program is held on Sunday and listened
> to by thousands of children. We have heard many remarks
> about the program, and one thing is certain, it didn't

---

46 Watts, Jill. *Mae West: an Icon in Black and White* Oxford University
    Press. 2001

Charlie McCarthy, Mae West

do Mae West, the program or the sponsor any good. Moreover, it has started a movement to have a League of Decency for radio similar to the one started several years ago for movies.[47]

Meanwhile, *The Los Angeles Times* presented a longer essay discussing the sketch, the public's reaction and the responsibility of entertainers on radio:

Nation-wide protests against the dialogue between Mae West, actress, and Charlie McCarthy, dummy of Edgar Bergen, on a coast-to-coast radio broadcast last Sunday, had reached such proportions last night that the National Broadcasting Company is reportedly preparing a formal apology to the public. Radio editors throughout the country have been swamped with a deluge of mail and telegrams protesting the conversation between the actress and the wooden stooge. It was learned from sources the first script designed for broadcasting was turned down as

47 League of Decency Planned For Radio. *Evening Vanguard.* December 15, 1937

too risqué and that a subsequent one was blue penciled for several hours before it was authorized for the air. Hollywood officials of the broadcasting company insisted that the script as finally approved contained no offensive feature. They added that it was the inflections at certain points in the dialogue which led to the protests. Answering reports that Miss West had "ad-libbed," Don Gilman, vice-president in charge of production, asserted Miss West followed her written lines. "Miss West adhered rigidly to the lines of the script," Gilman said. "It was the inflection she placed at certain points that has caused the furor of criticism. The whole situation is regrettable, but I am certain the objectionable features were solely a matter of interpretation," he added. Don Ameche, master of ceremonies, was asserted to have walked off the set when he became enraged at Miss West's inflections in the Adam and Eve comedy skit. "This same skit has been played over national radio programs on three previous occasions without any criticism," Gilman said. Miss West could not be reached last night, but officials of the film company which holds her contract came to her defense. "From the start, Miss West objected to the script," they said. "She wanted to play a part from her recent picture, but the producers of the show ruled otherwise. They insisted on the Adam and Eve skit. Miss West objected to it on the ground that anything connected with Adam and Eve is too closely associated with religion to be made into a comedy. If the program is condemned, then the producers should be blamed, not Miss West," they declared. Last night the J. Walter Thompson Advertising Company, representing the sponsor of the show, accepted responsibility for the script and expressed "our deepest and sincerest regrets." "It was a mistake and we can assure the public

Trade ad for Every Day's a Holiday

at large that the same error will not be made again," the company's statement said.[48]

The period articles refer to an Adam and Eve sketch which Mae performed with actor Don Ameche, where her Eve character considered Eden "a dump" and was quite eager to eat the apple of temptation. However, the biggest reaction came from the second half of the show when West had a verbal exchange with puppet Charlie McCarthy. Charlie was noted for being flirty with female

---

48   Row Stirred By Radio Skit. *Los Angeles Times*. December 17, 1937

guests as part of the act, but his banter with Mae was considered too suggestive. While lines like, "Come on home with me and I'll let you play in my wood pile," seem tame today, they caused an uproar in late 1937.

This sort of publicity could be good or bad, depending on the situation. But while Mae West had her supporters, the public at large was offended. Paramount released *Every Day's a Holiday* hoping that the film being much cleaner would result in moviegoers forgiving her, but they discovered the novelty of Mae West had worn off.

The film features Mae West as Peaches O'Day, a New York con artist in the 1890s. After getting in trouble with the law, Captain Jim McCarey (Edmund Lowe) of the police force lets her go with the condition that she leave town. Traveling to Boston, she becomes friends with the wealthy Van Reighle Van Doon (Charles Winninger) and his butler Graves (Charles Butterworth), and the three hatch a scheme thought up by Peaches' manager Nifty (Walter Catlett) that she return to New York disguised by a black wig and pass herself off as a French singer named Fifi. Police chief John Quade (Lloyd Nolan) tries to get "Fifi's" attention but gets nowhere. Humiliated, he orders McCarey to come up with reasons to close her show. When he refuses, he is stripped of his badge. Peaches goes to Quade's office and steals her police record. He and McCarey become wise to her, so Peaches convinces McCarey to run for Mayor against Quade.

There are a lot of familiar elements to *Every Day's a Holiday* that should allow it to fit comfortably among Mae West movies. It is set in the 19th century, Mae plays a cunning entertainer, and the men find her so striking they fall for the most outrageous cons – there is a very funny scene with her selling a hapless Herman Bing the Brooklyn Bridge that shows up early in the film. But there is little about Peaches that is suggestive in the same manner as Diamond Lil or any character she inspired. The dialog highlights and wordplay amount to little more than this exchange:

Walter Catlett, Mae West

Peaches O'Day: They got me all wrong. I might crack a law now and then, but I ain't never broke one.

Police Captain Jim McCarey: The only law you ain't never broke is the law of gravity.

This is amusing, but does not have the level of sharp wit found in films like *I'm No Angel* or *Klondike Annie.*

However, despite the cleaner approach to her humor, the controversy over the radio show with Bergen and McCarthy still loomed large. There was a cover article for the trade magazine Independent Exhibitors Film Bulletin that attempted to claim the controversy was blown out of proportion, stating:

When Mae West introduced Eve to the double entendre on a radio program several Sundays ago, she put on the spot a certain portion of the nation's exhibitors and her picture company, Paramount. The wide and diversified group we have questioned have unanimously answered that they found her performance mildly humorous and not offensive. As a matter of fact, none of these people ever gave a thought to the possibility that it might be

Mae West, Charles Butterworth

construed as irreligious or morally improper until they
subsequently read of the storm created by the broadcast. It is apparent that some circles of moviegoers have
been offended and are now more rabidly anti-West than
before. We may assume that, for the most part, these
are the same people who have never accepted her as a
fit subject to be purveyed as entertainment. Neverthe-
less, exhibitors operating theaters in communities largely
composed of the more moral-minded element should
not change the danger of incurring the ill-will of many
of their patrons by showing *Every Day's a Holiday*. There
is the threat here that the appearance of Mae West on
the screens of some theaters today will result in lasting
damage.[49]

While indicating that the reaction to Mae West's radio appearance was overdone, the trade still warned exhibitors about playing her latest picture, which hurt its box office. Meanwhile, a

---

49 The Mae West Situation. *Independent Exhibitors Film Bulletin.* January,
    1938

letter from one of those moviegoers to the magazine *Motion Picture* stated:

> I consider the recent dispute over Mae West's radio
> broadcast a lot of good old-fashioned bunk. The sooner
> the whole thing is forgotten the better off everyone will
> be. The only reason I am writing this letter is to let Miss
> West know that not everyone is against her. Mae West in
> *Every Day's a Holiday* was shown recently in Indianapolis
> and was the first West picture not held over for a second
> or third week. It is very unfortunate that the protest,
> resulting from the broadcast, had to happen, for surely
> that is what kept so many of the patrons from the theater.
> I did my part for my favorite movie actress, for I saw the
> picture three times downtown and intend to see it again
> when it comes to the neighborhood theaters. I hope the
> picture does well at the box office in other cities for the
> longer Miss West is on the screen the happier all of her
> loyal fans will be.

This letter, written by Harold R. Daringer of Indianapolis, Indiana, won a $5 prize from the magazine, but it did not help the film's box office numbers.

Undaunted, Cohen sent West out on a ten week tour to promote the film, and Mae enjoyed resurrecting her vaudeville act with none of the restrictions imposed upon her by Breen and the movie industry. But it was evident that Breen had won. Her style was limited by the parameters forced upon her work, while any risqué material was wildly condemned. Retaining a fan base in some quarters, Mae West was no longer the exciting new box office success she had been a few years earlier. Exhibitors sent in pretty caustic reports from their audiences:

> Let's hope this is the last of West. A flop. People don't
> care to see West, and they tell you by staying away. I
> want no more of them.

Didn't do much business on it and was glad of it. Pass it if you can; you can get better pictures than this one and you'll never miss it. Won't get you a dime over expenses and you're lucky if you break even.[50]

A review in the trade magazine *Picture Play* offered an unimpressed but accepting reaction, wishing for the Mae West of earlier films:

It is no longer smart for any self-respecting critic to find anything to praise in a Mae West picture, but I still like the old gal. I think she's foxy. Naturally her pictures haven't the same old-time and bold innuendo of, say, *She Done Him Wrong*. The purity leagues and others have cramped her style. Which is as well, or there is no telling how far she could have gone. She's foxy in putting on a good show in spite of censorship.[51]

By the Spring of 1938, Mae West found herself on a list in the *Hollywood Reporter* of several actresses who had once been top stars and were now considered "box office poison." However, Emmanuel Cohen noted that her personal appearances were packed with Mae West fans and believed the actress still had a lot to offer. He offered her several scripts but she rejected them all, still insisting on playing Catherine the Great. Cohen had other problems as well. A rift between him and Paramount president Adolph Zukor resulted in the studio dropping their distribution deal for his productions. Of course, this meant that the stars signed with him were also dropped from the studio including Mae West. West and Cohen parted ways, and Mae went back out on tour, telling the press that she intended to film her script about Catherine the Great with her own funds.

Returning from the tour, Mae West was contacted by Universal studios to co-star with W.C. Fields in a feature film, which she would co-write and co-star. The money was good and West badly needed a hit. Fields had just left Paramount a year earlier after

50 What The Picture Did For Me. *Motion Picture Herald.* April 16, 1938.
51 Every Day's a Holiday review. *Picture Play.* October, 1938

Mae West with black wig as Fifi

appearing in *The Big Broadcast of 1938*. His drinking and health issues had become so concerning, he was off screen for all of 1937, biding his time in radio with, ironically Edgar Bergen and Charlie McCarthy. Fields did some of his best work with the duo, and when he was hired at Universal in 1939, his first film there, *You Can't Cheat an Honest Man* featured them and was a box office hit. Universal execs felt a teaming with the now-available Mae West would result in the good film and good box office. Both West and Fields agreed and began writing the screenplay for what would become *My Little Chickadee*.

MY LITTLE CHICKADEE

Directed by Edward F. Cline
Screenplay by Mae West, W.C. Fields
Produced by Lester Cowan
Cinematography by Joseph A. Valentine
Film Editing by Edward Curtiss

Song:
Willie of the Valley
Lyrics by Milton Drake
Music by Ben Oakland

Cast:
Mae West.....................Flower Belle Lee
W.C. Fields ....Cuthbert J. Twillie
Joseph Calleia..................Jeff Badger
Dick Foran....................Wayne Carter
Ruth Donnelly.................Aunt Lou
Margaret Hamilton ....Mrs. Gideon
Donald Meek..................Amos Budge
Fuzzy Knight ....Cousin Zeb
Willard Robertson ....Uncle John
George Moran ....Milton
William Benedict...............Lem
George Melford ....Greasewood
Fay Adler ....Mrs. 'Pygmy' Allen
Gene Austin...................Saloon Musician
Russell Hall ....Candy
Otto Heimel...................Coco
Jimmy Conlin.................Squawk Mulligan
Otto Hoffman ....Pete
Addison Richards...............Judge

Georgie Billings . . . . Boy
Jackie Searl. . . . . Boy
Delmar Watson . . . . Boy
Clyde Dembeck . . . . Small Boy on Train
Jan Duggan . . . . Uppity Little Bend Woman
Wade Boteler . . . . Leading Citizen
James C. Mortonw . . . . Train Conductor
Al Ferguson . . . . Train Passenger
Chester Gan. . . . . Chinese Train Passenger
Anne Nagel . . . . Miss Ermingarde Foster -
                                              Schoolteacher
Ben Hall. . . . . Schoolboy
Charles Hart . . . . Schoolboy
Danny Jackson . . . . Schoolboy
Buster Slaven . . . . Schoolboy
William Davidson . . . . Sheriff of Little Bend
Si Jenks. . . . . Deputy
Harlan Briggs. . . . . Hotel Clerk
Lane Chandler . . . . Porter
Buddy Harris . . . . Porter
Lita Chevret. . . . . Indian squaw
J.C. Fowler . . . . Dinner Party Guest
Dorothy Vernon . . . . Dinner Party Guest
Slim Gaut. Bowlegged Man
Kit Guard. Reports Twillie's Story
Bill Nestell . . . . Lynch Mob Member
Betty Roche . . . . Salvation Army Girl
Dick Rush . . . . Stage Guard
Vester Pegg. . . . . Gambler
Morgan Wallace . . . . Gambler
Jack Roper . . . . Henchman
Bing Conley . . . . Henchman
John Kelly. Henchman
Sailor Vincent . . . . Henchman
Eddie Butler. . . . . Henchman

Al Bridge . . . . Barfly Drinking Straight Whiskey
Edward Hearn . . . . Barfly Drinking Panther
Bill Wolfe. . . . . Barfly in Trance
Al Haskell . . . . Barfly
Bob Burns . . . . Barfly
Carl Sepulveda . . . . Townsman
Blackie Whiteford . . . . Townsman
Joe Whitehead . . . . Townsman
Mark Anthony . . . . Townsman
John Barton . . . . Townsman
Hank Bell. . . . . Townsman
Tex Phelps . . . . Townsman
Bob Reeves. . . . . Townsman
Paul Kruger . . . . Townsman
Philo McCullough . . . . Townsman
Walter McGrail . . . . Townsman
Robert McKenzie. . . . . Townsman
Charles McMurphy . . . . Townsman
George Huggins. . . . . Townsman
Lloyd Ingraham . . . . Townsman
Herman Hack . . . . Townsman
Robert Haines . . . . Townsman
Frank Ellis . . . . Townsman
Victor Cox . . . . Townsman
Nora Bush . . . . Townswoman

Released March 15, 1940
Universal Studios
Running time: 83 minutes

When Mae West returned from touring with her show and was approached by Universal for a movie with W.C. Fields, she didn't have many other options. She had not only become controversial in a much different era than the one welcoming a movie like *I'm*

Mae West as Flower Belle in My Little Chickadee

No Angel, she also was named "box office poison" in a major trade magazine.

Mae West and W.C. Fields were very similar in many ways. Both had come from vaudeville, both challenged the ways and mores of cultural society with their comedy, and both insisted on meticulous control of their work. The studio felt that the two of them would be kindred spirits and collaborate effectively as a result.

Although W.C. Fields and Mae West both spent many years at Paramount during the early and mid 1930s, and their dressing rooms were next to each other, they never appeared in a film together. Fields came up with an idea shortly after a Masquers testimonial dinner celebrating his 40th anniversary in show business. and wrote a script called *December and Mae,* which featured the two of them as a couple of grifters not unlike he and Alison Skipworth had played in the Paramount pre-code films *If I Had a Million* (1932) and *Tillie and Gus* (1933). Fields submitted a draft of the script entitled *December and Mae* which was reworked

W.C. Fields, Mae West

by screenwriter Grover Jones. Jones was a versatile writer who penned action adventure movies like *Souls at Sea* (1937), comedies like the Harold Lloyd vehicle *The Milky Way* (1936) and the John Wayne western *Dark Command* (1940), before his career was cut short by his death in 1940.

Fields was the bigger star at this time, enjoying one of the strongest periods of his career, while Mae West was "box office poison." And each was a solo performer who did not "team" with anyone, nor did either like to work from a prepared script. West, however, saw the film as an opportunity to secure funds for a self-financed production about Catherine the Great.

Fields did not like Grover Jones' script at all, believing it tamed his established screen persona and missed West's all together, pointing out a scene where Mae is sewing. West, however, liked Jones' script as a basis and planned to write her own material to formulate a screenplay. Fields would then create the scenes for his character and it was Jones who would figure out how to blend the two perspectives into a cohesive narrative. Meanwhile, the Breen office was alerted that two performers who were known for challenging censorship rules were now co-writing and co-starring in a film. However, the resulting script was clean enough so that only a few minor areas of West's portion needed to be reworked (including a romance with a Native American).

An article in the trade magazine *Hollywood* promoted the teaming of Mae West and W.C. Fields as truly inspired casting:

> With great bravery, Universal is making a picture called *My Little Chickadee* starring a wicked blond lady named Miss Mae West and a man who will kick a baby in the slats for a laugh, W.C. Fields. If *My Little Chickadee* can snake through the Hays office without having its innuendos clipped, the public is in for some hilarity and wild laughter. This picure is what is coyly known as a superwestern and it is replete in scenes calculated to give Mr. Hays and Mr. Breen harrowing existences. Men sneak in and out of the blond lady's bedroom, there is a bogus marriage, a song about a man chased by women for the gold in his teeth, Indian fights, and a mob that has its mind set on lynching Mr. Fields for card-sharping. The Hays establishment has okayed the script, but it is going to look a nervous breakdown in the face just the same, mostly because there is no telling about the blond lady. She is a problem, this lady is. What she's got won't go into scripts. She has the most eloquent gait in the animal kingdom. When this lady walks, scripts burn. Besides that, she has a voice that overwhelms descriptions. When it comes to saying words the way they shouldn't be said, the lady is just plain breathtaking.[52]

My Little Chickadee is still essentially a series of scenes, some involving West, others involving Fields. The Mae West footage is basically a western story in which a masked bandit (Joseph Calleia) not only terrorizes the town, but also romances the town beauty Flower Belle. And as Flower Belle, West exudes the persona she had established on stage and in her early Paramount films. She

---

52 Riley, Thomas Nord. Battle of the Sexes. *Hollywood.* 1940

Ad for My Little Chickadee

remains completely unflappable despite the level of danger, purring her dialog and carrying herself about in a flirtatious manner. Fields is also his usual screen persona as Cuthbert J. Twillie, but his tricky nature is caught off guard when Flower Belle talks him into pretending to be her husband as they each roll into a western town where the masked bandit is flourishing. She hopes their phony marriage (performed by a gambler posing as a minister), will give her some level of respectability in her new town.

Neither actor's scenes dominated the production. West unflappably saunters through each of her sequences, engaging in such highlights as being asked to spend the day running the local school room, discovering that the hick boy students are smarter than she is. It doesn't matter, as she charms her way through the day, responding to the ogling boys in her usual manner. The boys whistle at her, she smirks, "there'll be no more of that" with a sly wink. She looks over the sentences on the blackboard which state: "I am a good boy." "I am a good man." "I am a good girl," then responding, "What is this, propaganda?" During her sequence teaching the class, she gives such lessons as, "Two and two is four and five will get you ten if you know how to work it."

Fields is typically quite funny as the con man Twillie, duping a gambler out of $100 in gold during a game of high card cut, and waxing nostalgic about past days as a bartender when he knocked down the notorious Chicago Molly. Jimmy Conlin, as fellow bartender Squawk is nearby.

> Twillie: You remember when I knocked down Chicago Molly.
>
> Squawk: You knocked her down? I was the one who knocked her down!
>
> Twillie: Yeah, but I was the one who started kicking her!
>
> Squawk: Then she came back the next night and beat us both up
>
> Twillie: Yeah, but she had a another woman with her.

Mae West, W.C. Fields

In another highlight, Twillie disguises himself as the masked bandit and goes to Flower Belle's room with romance as the intent. He ends up captured and sentenced to be hanged. When asked for any last requests, Twillie states, "Yes, I'd like to see Paris before I die." And then, as the noose tightens around his neck: "I'll settle for Philadelphia."

The film concludes with Flower Belle clearing Twillie's name and wrapping up her business with the masked bandit. In true Mae West movie fashion, her character also leaves behind a broken hearted newspaper editor (Dick Foran) who has fallen for her. As Flower Belle and Twillie part company for the last time, Fields and West burlesque each other. Twillie invites Flower Belle to "come up and see me some time," whereupon Flora Belle responds playfully with, "Ah yes, I'll do that my little chickadee."

Fields and West offered this playful cuteness to their on screen relationship throughout the film. He is nothing like the type of character West falls for – he was not handsome and in control, but a comical con man whom she could handily manipulate. This is balanced by the presence of Calleia's and Foran's characters. Twillie and Flower Belle's first meeting offers this amusing exchange:

> Twillie: May I present my card?
>
> Flower Belle: 'Novelties and Notions.' What kind of notions you got?
>
> Twillie: You'd be surprised. Some are old, some are new. Whom have I the honor of addressing, m'lady?
>
> Flower Belle: They call me Flower Belle.
>
> Twillie: What a euphonious appellation. Easy on the ears and a banquet for the eyes.
>
> Flower Belle: You're kinda cute yourself.
>
> Twillie: Thank you. I never argue with a lady.
>
> Flower Belle Lee: Smart boy.

Fields and West got along well during pre-production, agreeing that she would receive top billing as star and screenwriter if he was allowed to choose their director. Fields wanted A. Edward Sutherland, which pleased Mae because she got along well with him while shooting her last Paramount film, *Every Day's a Holiday,* which he had directed. Sutherland was busy on another project, so Fields then asked for Eddie Cline, with West's support. Cline directed the film.

Because Fields was the biggest star, and signed with Universal, most of the publicity during production concentrated on him. Hedda Hopper's column stated:

> W.C. Fields, who ad-libs all over the place, was going good the other day on *My Little Chickadee* when his scene was (according to the script) over. But Fields kept right on, and Director Eddie Cline let the cameras grind.[53]

An angry West spouted off on the set, "Someone oughta tell Hedda Hopper I'm in this picture too."

---

53 Hedda Hopper's Hollywood. *The Los Angeles Times.* November 16, 1939

W.C. Fields, Mae West

As a result, West started telling the press that she wrote the film and Fields merely made a few fleeting contributions. This was a bit much for the Fields ego, so he called her "a plumber's version of Cleopatra." This conflict continued long after Fields' 1946 death. When his movies became popular among high school and college students during the late 1960s and early 1970s, Mae West was alive and making appearances, and became annoyed when constantly being asked about "the W.C. Fields movie she was in."

My Little Chickadee received mixed reviews but grossed over $2 million against a $625,000 budget. Most of the critics compared it unfavorably to another western parody released about the same time, Fritz Lang's *Destry Rides Again* (1939). Fields would go on to make *The Bank Dick* (1940), which remains one of the best films of his entire career. According to film critic and scholar Katie Carter:

> A lot of reviews at the time praised Fields but criticized West, even though both were parodying their established screen personas equally in this movie. West's double entendres are still a bit watered down as they were in her other post-Code films, but a lot of them still land (namely the schoolhouse scene) and it was clearly enough to rile the censors somewhat— especially since a lot of what plot there is, or at least the back-and-forth between West and Field's characters, revolves around sex.

Because of the box office success of *My Little Chickadee,* Universal wanted to sign Mae West to a contract for more films. MGM offered her a role opposite Wallace Beery. A spy story opposite John Barrymore was proposed by RKO.

Mae West continued to work on her script about Catherine the Great, now wanting to make it as a major film in Technicolor. It wasn't until 1943 that West was back on screen in a new movie. Her friend Gregory Ratoff arranged for a musical at Columbia entitled *The Heat's On* with Mae West as its star.

THE HEAT'S ON

Directed by Gregory Ratoff
Screenplay by Fitzroy Davis, George S. George, Fred Schiller from
a story by Lou Breslow, Boris Ingster.
Produced by Gregory Ratoff
Cinematography by Franz Planer
Film Editing by Franz Planer

Songs:
I'm Just a Stranger in Town
Music by Jay Gorney
Lyrics by Henry Myers and Edward Eliscu

There Goes That Guitar
Music by Jay Gorney
Lyrics by Henry Myers and Edward Eliscu

Antonio
Music by John Blackburn
Lyrics by Fabian Andre

The White Keys and the Black Keys
Music by Jay Gorney
Lyrics by Henry Myers and Edward Eliscu

Thinkin' About the Wabash
Music by Jule Styne
Lyrics by Sammy Cahn

Caisson Song
Music and Lyrics by Edmund L. Gruber

They Looked So Pretty on the Envelope
Music by Jay Gorney
Lyrics by Henry Myers and Edward Eliscu

Hello, Mi Amigo
Music by Jay Gorney
Lyrics by Henry Myers and Edward Eliscu

Cast:

Mae West . . . . Fay Lawrence
Victor Moore . . . . Hubert Bainbridge
William Gaxton . . . . Tony Ferris
Lester Allen . . . . Mouse Beller
Alan Dinehart . . . . Forrest Stanton
Mary Roche . . . . Janey Adair
Lloyd Bridges . . . . Andy Walker
Almira Sessions . . . . Hannah Bainbridge
Sam Ash . . . . Frank
David Lichine . . . . Specialty Dancer
Leonard Sues . . . . Trumpet Player
Jack Owens . . . . Jack
Joan Thorsen . . . . Singer
Hazel Scott . . . . Organ Player
Xavier Cugat . . . . Orchestra Leader
Leon Belasco . . . . Shore - the Agent
Beatrice Blinn . . . . Babette
Boyd Davis . . . . Dr. H. Snyder
Roy Engel . . . . Roy
Harry Harvey . . . . Harry
Lina Romay . . . . Lina
Leo Mostovoy . . . . Mac - the Headwaiter
Harry Shannon . . . . Police Captain
John Sheehan . . . . Police Officer Closing the
                                              Show
Alex Romero . . . . Dancer

Joanne Frank . . . . Showgirl
Eddie Hall . . . . Singer
Donald Kerr . . . . Stage Manager
Ray Teal . . . . Stagehand
Harry Tyler . . . . Stagehand
Edward Earle . . . . Writer
Colin Kenny . . . . Nightclub Patron
Harold Miller . . . . Nightclub Patron
Cosmo Sardo . . . . Nightclub Patron

Released December 2, 1943
Gregory Ratoff Productions
Columbia Pictures
Running time: 79 minutes

After the success of *My Little Chickadee* resulted in renewed interest in Mae West, she felt her idea for a film on Catherine the Great may get some traction. An article in Robbin Coons' syndicated column stated:

> Mae West like her own heroine Diamond Lil is "doin' a job she never done before" She's c'ming up to see the Russians sometime — and soon. "Now's the time" she said "The Russians are doin' some marvelous fightin' and everybody's interested in Russia so I've decided to do it. It's a picture I've been dreamin' about a long time." The picture is a yarn of Catherine the Great or "Catherine Was Great" as she'll call it. Once she planned it as a $2,000,000 spectacle in color. That's out now "We'll make the scenes more intimate instead of spectacular," she said. Mae has been boning up on the Catherine era. Mae plans to play Catherine straight - a character without Mae West touches. "I've had some pretty wonderful dramatic training," said Mae "and I'm goin' to use it. I couldn't have played Diamond Lil without that training. Lil was a

queen and Catherine was just another queen on a higher plane".

While Mae continued to pursue the Catherine project, the spy story from RKO looked promising. She liked the script by Andrew Stone and Fred Jackson, in which she played a spy who goes to Berlin "to take care of Hitler." Mae further stated:

> I knew that "come up and see me sometime" and "you can be had, big boy" couldn't go on, but that's what the public wants. Well, I gave it to em until everybody in show business was imitating my stuff. That's when I started turning down pictures. They said I was being difficult.[54]

Mae indicated that she was interested in exploring her acting abilities beyond the screen persona she had established. But the spy film at RKO never did get made.

While offscreen, Mae's name remained in the press. She lobbied for the warden of San Quentin, Clinton Duffy, to remain in his position. Among her fan mail were several letters from inmates, all of who praised the warden, prompting Mae to write the governor of California, Culbert Olson, stating:

> "I hope your excellency will feel as I do and let Warden Duffy continue making bad men good while I continue making good men bad — I mean in my pictures" In reply the governor expressed his appreciation in Miss West's "interest in Warden Duffy's efforts to make bad men good even though it was not you who made them bad. You may be assured that the work of rehabilitation of prisoners to which our present prison management is devoted and which is being so successfully carried on at San Quentin by Warden Duffy will continue during my administration."[55]

---

54   Erskine Johnson column. Syndicated. November 5, 1942
55   Olson Bandies Letters with Mae West. *The Sacramento Union.* January 22, 1941

Mae West in The Heat's On

As America entered World War Two, Mae was tickled to find that the Navy named its life preservers after her. An irksome development was her marriage to Frank Wallace that continued to plague her, and which she continued to deny until Wallace sued for separate maintenance. West made a settlement with Wallace in 1942 which allowed her to obtain a divorce.

When it was finally set that Mae West was returning to movies after a three year absence, the press talked about Gregory Ratoff's new musical for Columbia, initially titled *Tropicana*. West continued to indicate that she was interested in expanding beyond her established screen persona:

> The lady of the arched eyebrow, the curled lip and the curved hip the prototype of the Belle of the Nineties has been streamlined for a snappy defense age. The actress who slinked across America's screens with a knowing nod of the head and twinkle in the eye is back in an entirely new personality - done up for America at war. Yes, Mae West is dressed up to the minute. The siren of the Gay Nineties returns to films as the ambassadress of goodwill in *Tropicana* which Gregory Ratoff produces and directs for Columbia release, with Victor Moore, William Gaxton and Hazel Scott. It has been over two years since Mae West appeared in pictures. At that time, she played opposite W.C. Fields in *My Little Chickadee* as the last in a long cycle of turn of the century belles. Then Mae West left pictures for a while in spite of the strident clamor of loyal fans' and repeated urgings of agents, producers and filmmakers. The reason for over two years of absence? Let the lady speak for herself. "You can do a good thing just so many times before people begin to ask themselves, 'Where have I seen that before?' Well, that's the way I felt about my Diamond Lil characterization. I played the same role in nine pictures. Then, after completing my ninth, they handed me more scripts with Diamond Lil. I figured that the public had seen enough of that one portrayal, and I felt I wanted to do something different . Since making my last picture almost a dozen scripts have been offered to me all of them were Diamond Lil. You know it's a funny thing. When I first came to Hollywood and wanted to do *She Done Him Wrong*, they told me that the fans would never go for that period stuff. The modem generation wanted something zippy and new. Well, the success of the formula proved that I was right. Diamond Lil went over with a bang. And now Im just as convinced

Ad for The Heat's On

that I shouldn't repeat it a 10th time. I believe that my role in *Tropicana* will prove' that was right" In Columbia's *Tropicana*, Mae West plays the part of a celebrated Broadway stage actress who journeys across the border on a goodwill tour. The story is modern and is given a completely modem treatment.[56]

Unfortunately, for all the ballyhoo that preceded it, *The Heat's On* was not a successful introduction of a new Mae West. In fact, it managed to dismantle the interest generated by the success of *My*

---

56   Mae West is Back Again. *Los Angeles Daily News*. July 8, 1943

Little Chickadee. Firstly, for all of the claims in the press that West was interested in expanding her horizons as an actress, she was furious when she read the script and saw that her character was a temperamental has-been actress struggling to deal with a younger woman taking her spot. That was a bit too far from Diamond Lil for Mae's tastes, and she told Ratoff she wouldn't do the movie. Ratoff had already shot several musical numbers for the film, and had backers he needed to appease. He convinced Mae to take the role, but only after agreeing she could rewrite her character and her dialog. This altered the screenplay's narrative significantly. Mae was used to penning the entire screenplay, so just writing her character within the parameters of someone else's script did not mesh with the rest of what had been written. This caused rewrites throughout the filming of the movie.

The story features Broadway producer Tony Ferris (William Gaxton) in financial trouble regarding his latest show. This causes the show's star, Fay Lawrence (Mae West), to consider working for Tony's rival Forrest Stanton (Alan Dinehart). Tony concocts a scheme to generate publicity by telling stuffy Hubert Bainbridge (Victor Moore) that his show is dirty. Bainbridge is currently heading a foundation that intends to clean up Broadway so he has the show raided. Tony believes this publicity will generate interest, but soon the show is closed and Fay goes to work for Stanton in the show *Tropicana.* Tony comes up with another scheme, agreeing to cast Bainbridge's singer niece Janey (Mary Roche) as the star of his next show, then tells Stanton that Fay has been blacklisted, and agrees to buy *Tropicana* to cut Stanton's losses, convincing Bainbridge to finance the show. Fay uses her feminine charm to get Bainbridge to admit to Tony's scheme, and lets Stanton know. Bainbridge's sister Hannah, who was away on business but is the true head of the Foundation, is notified by Stanton, and she shows up at the theater to take immediate action. She dismisses Janey, tells Hubert to return to his menial job in the foundation, and tells Tony she has frozen his accounts. Feigning insanity, Tony tells Fay he went crazy due to all this trouble and she agrees to

Mae West, Victor Moore

take over the show. Fay confronts Hannah and states that she will expose Hubert's embezzlement activities unless she finances the show. It becomes a success.

Reviewer Fred Stengel of the trade magazine *Motion Picture Daily* reviewed *The Heat's On* in the magazine's November 29, 1943 issue:

> Somewhere along the line the heat was turned off and this picture went wide off the mark. Personalities who are capable of better acting with stronger material and more inspired direction are stymied in *The Heat's On*. This is the first picture Miss West has made in the past three years. There has been no change of style in the interval.[57]

---

57 Stengel, Fred. The Heat's On review. *Motion Picture Daily.* November 29, 1943

The review in another trade magazine, *Film Daily*, had similar misgivings about this Mae West comeback, calling the film "a mild musical":

> The heat isn't on long enough in this film to warm up the paying customers sufficiently to warrant any more than a lukewarm reaction. Although the intentions were apparently good, the picture misfires badly. If the film fails to make its mark, it cannot be said to be any lack of drawing names. The trouble is that the scriptwriters and director have not been able to extract the best from this talent available to them. The film possesses just about enough good moments to get by in the neighborhood theaters. Miss West doesn't come up to expectations, overdoing the part of a wordly-wise musical comedy star of the hard boiled school.[58]

The chief problem with *The Heat's On* is that it doesn't seem like a Mae West movie at all. It is just a rather standard musical in which Mae West happens to appear in a role. And her presence seems like a watered down throwback; a wartime version of a pre-code character. The chief highlights are some of the musical numbers, including Lina Romay with Xavier Cugat's orchestra, and Hazel Scott's dual piano number "The White Keys and the Black Keys." Regarding Scott, Mae noticed how things had changed in the past few years for Black performers. Hazel dined freely and comfortably with the rest of the cast, when only six years earlier Mae aroused controversy for daring to have lunch with Louis Armstrong on the set of *Every Day's a Holiday*.

In her autobiography, Mae West stated: "After this dismal experience I made up my mind that I would never do another picture unless everything, but everything, was to my satisfaction, and so stipulated in black and white, without an accent."[59] Film critic and scholar Katie Carter stated:

---

58 The Heat's On review. *Film Daily.* December 3, 1943
59 West, Mae. *Goodness Had Nothing To Do With It.* Avon. 1959

Regardless of what contributions she did or didn't have to her character in the script, you can tell this project isn't really hers. And she's also barely in the movie, perhaps appearing for about a quarter of its runtime. Individually, the music numbers are impressive, especially Scott's. But the whole affair is rather dull, and those music breaks aren't edited so well into what narrative there is.[60]

The Heat's On ended up being the last movie Mae West was in for another 27 years. But she never strayed too far from the spotlight and worked regularly for the remainder of the 1940s and throughout the 1950s and 1960s.

---

60 Author's assistant

MAE WEST IN THE 40s, 50s, 60s

After *The Heat's On* Mae West moved away from motion pictures and concentrated on other projects for which she had full creative control. Mae had created quite a legacy, and despite being past 50, she still had significant appeal, especially from those who remembered her best films of ten years earlier, and had known about her legendary stage appearances. Mae had spent a career flirting with edgy material, engaging in veiled sexual content, and

John Carradine, Mae West, John Barrymore

battling the censors on several levels. Having cleaned up her act in movies, her last film appearance in *The Heat's On* was too much of a departure, and she was on screen too little for being the film's star. Mae was not limited to films. She always realized she could return to the stage.

Of course, her first venture was to finally bring *Catherine Was Great* to the stage after years of unsuccessfully trying to get it made into a movie. West had become interested in various aspects of spirituality at around this time, and would claim that the spirit of Catherine the Great instructed her to approach this role with great seriousness and commitment. Mae secured the services of producer Mike Todd, later known for widescreen cinema and the Oscar winning 1956 feature *Around The World in Eighty Days,* as well as being married to Elizabeth Taylor when he was killed in a plane crash in 1958.

Catherine Was Great, buoyed by the presence of Mae West as the star of a self-written play, ran a successful 191 performances on Broadway, first at the Shubert Theater and next at the Royale. It then went on a successful tour. John Chapman, theater critic for *The New York Daily News* stated in his review:

> Last night the impetuous and pecunious Michael Todd
> presented Miss West and her *Catherine Was Great* at the
> Shubert Theatre…. The result is an overpowering what-
> not, a curio…. It has long been known that Mae West,
> the actress, has curves, and her long absence from stage
> and screen seems not to have impaired them. Last night
> it became apparent that Mae West, the playwright, also
> has curves, billows, swells, swirls and curlicues. Her prose
> has the pomp of the changing of the guards ceremony at
> Buckingham Palace. She and the cast of 50 or 60 with
> whom she has surrounded herself speak in prose which
> is not only measured but also weighted; and when, as
> empress, she commands a valet, "Get me a traveling case
> and my peasant disguise" then, oh boy, you know she is
> cooking on the front burner. This come up and see me

some time biography of the Empress of all the Russians, played as hoke drama, could have provided an evening's laughter in a simple Hoboken beer hall in prohibition. Even now there is Borne laughter in it, for Miss West's throaty manner of tossing away lines and her wonderful simplification of the subtleties of sex are still effective. But not all of *Catherine Was Great* is played for laughs. Not enough of it. Long stretches are cloak-and-sword melo-drama, slowed by the necessity of giving Miss West every possible stellar advantage. Her every entrance is a parade, even when she comes in all by herself, which is not often. The plot, as you can imagine, is a series of conquests one or two of them military, the rest amatory. As Miss West said in a curtain speech to an audience which had given her a really warm personal welcome, "Catherine had 300 lovers. I did the best I could in a couple of hours." If she had, in the play, maintained the frame of mind of this speech, "Catherine" would have been better.[61]

The play had barely opened before it was hit with a lawsuit by writers George S. George and Vadim Uraneff who claimed they had written the play with West back in the late 1930s when she was developing it as a film. She was later sued by another pair of writers, Edwin K. O'Brien and Michael Karr, who claimed they also provided material. Mae, of course, denied all of this, indicating she was always the author of her plays, but the suits were eventually settled.

After *Catherine Was Great* completed its run, Mae was ready to put together another show she had penned, this one entitled *Come On Up*. The press stated:

Mae West will appear in her new stage vehicle, *Come On Up* at the Auditorium on Monday and Tuesday, Nov. 4 and 5. In the past Miss West has stirred interest in almost every stage production she has appeared in. In her new

---

61 Chapman, John. Mae West Gives History The 0-0 In Lavish Catherine Was Great. *New York Daily News.*August 4, 1944

Mae West as Catherine the Great

offering, the star of stage and screen depicts a character of the 'Mae West type' the kind that made her widely known. The story of her new ploy has Mexico City and post-war Washington as backgrounds, and is the combined efforts of the late Miles Mander, Fred Schiller and Thomas Dunphy. The entire production was staged by

Russell Fillmore. Miss West is supported by a company of 30 people.[62]

Mae toured with *Come On Up* at the end of 1945 and into 1946, but it was far less successful than *Catherine Was Great.* Bob Thomas, in his syndicated column, was not only dismissive of this show, he called Mae a has-been in so many words:

> Mae West is back In town with a wheezing bit of theatrical claptrap called *Come On Up.* The Jane Russell of the 30s managed to squeeze a lot of laughs out of the first-nighters.[63]

While his comments were somewhat veiled, comparing her to the then-popular Jane Russell (most notable at the time for the controversial film *The Outlaw*), and pinpointing the 1930s, relegated Mae West to someone who used to be something comparable to a current star. This show's lack of success prompted Mae to revive *Diamond Lil* for the stage.

Despite her work on Broadway, West's notoriety in the mainstream was decidedly slipping. A letter to the editor Fresno newspaper in August of 1949, ostensibly from a younger person, asked, "Why is Mae West so popular?" Mae's last hit movie had been nine years earlier, so her mentions in the press and lack of mainstream exposure apparently made her notoriety confusing to younger people.

The revival of *Diamond Lil* was supposed to be a throwback and was accepted as such. It was Mae's intention to remind people of a past accomplishment that continued to define her career. John Chapman's review in *The New York Daily News* stated:

> It is the same old Mae in the same old play and now it
> is funnier and so is she. Its extravagant sexiness and its
> background of Bowery dives, swan beds, white slavery
> and hoodlumism were spoofs even in 1928, but the cynicism of the play and its star rather pleasantly naughty. On

---

62 Mae West Due Nov. 4. *Democrat and Chronicle* Rochester, NY. October 20, 1946

63 Bob Thomas syndicated column. Associated Press February 17 1947

the strength of one of the curtain lines "Come up and see me some time," Hollywood asked Miss West to come out and teach the movie how to get away with the single entendre instead of the double entendre. She went and taught. Now she is back to instruct another generation of playgoers, and she doesn't look or act a day older or better. Saturday evening's premiere was an event, with a platoon of cops keeping a big gallery of gawkers across the street. Miss West was hot -- much hotter than she was 20 years ago.[64]

The revival of *Diamond Lil* was a positive way for Mae West to close out the decade of the 1940s. As she entered the 1950s, there were more stage shows and other such activities, but she continued to stay away from movies. She got offers. Notably she was asked to play the Norma Desmond role in Billy Wilder's *Sunset Boulevard* (1950) with Marlon Brando planned as her co-star, but she immediately rejected the idea of playing a has-been. Gloria Swanson and William Holden ended up famously playing the leads. In 1951, producers wanted her to co-star with Jane Russell in a film called *Mother Knows Best*. Producer Jerry Wald spoke to Mae on the phone and tried to convince her to take the role, insisting she would be playing Jane's sister, not mother. But she still refused. That same year, a traveling show of *Diamond Lil* was banned in Atlanta as being too lewd. Just like the old days.

One of the more intriguing movie ideas offered Mae, and one that she was seriously considering, was a comedy set in the gay nineties where she'd star opposite Bob Hope. However, negotiations broke down when Hope felt the script centered more on the female lead rather than his role. Meanwhile, Mae continued to be quoted in the press with lines like "I won't go on television until it gets bigger proportions," and "I don't like reading. I have to take off my eyelashes to put on my glasses."

---

64 Chapman, John. Diamond Lil review. *The New York Daily News*. February 7, 1949

Mae West took her act to nightclubs in the 1950s

In early 1953, Mae was announced as being signed for the film *Pal Joey*, which was to be directed by Billy Wilder. Columnists syndicated in newspapers were not enthusiastic when they announced this news, many indicating her last film was ten years earlier and was a box office flop. Her best movie work was 20 years earlier. Eventually it was announced that Marlon Brando would be the male star. However, Columbia Pictures studio head nixed this project on paper and it wasn't until 1957 when *Pal Joey* was made, and starred Frank Sinatra instead of Brando, Rita Hayworth rather than Mae West, and was directed by George Sidney. Mae would state in a 1954 interview: "I was offered the matron's role in *Pal Joey* opposite Marlon Brando, but I turned it down. Joe makes a sucker of the dame and that's against my whole concept of handling men.[65]

In 1954, Mae West decided to take her act to nightclubs, debuting at the Sahara in Las Vegas on July 27th. Hedda Hopper interviewed Mae for her syndicated column:

> The nuclear scientists with their atom bomb tests rattled windows and doors in Las Vegas but when Mae West ambles on the stage at the Sahara July 27 and sings "I Like to Do All Day What I Do All Night" as an opener and "Take It Easy, Boys, and Last a Long, Long Time" for an encore, the whole town will shake. In her apartment, within yelling distance of Hollywood and Vine, she was, as usual, surrounded by men. Six photographers were working to get new shots of the Empress of Sex. "Always do my best acting on a couch," she announced in that sultry voice. She's the same old Mae, hand on hip and tongue in cheek, kidding the pants off sex. She looks just as she did when W. C. Fields called her his "little chickadee." For a rollicking half-hour, she had me and the bulb boys splitting our sides over her quick comebacks and characteristic intonations. I asked, "why have you never

---

65 Bacon, James. More Women Than Men Come to See Mae. Syndicated. Associated Press. December 6, 1954

appeared in a night club before?" "I never cared to entertain people while they're dining," she said. "If anybody lifts a bite of food to his mouth while this one is on stage, it'll be a minor miracle."[66]

The nightclub tour was a big success, audiences excited to see the uncensored show of the entertainer who had reached superstar status, even without having made a movie in over ten years. At a stop in Buffalo, a reporter asked how she stayed so fit and attractive:

I've been giving that some thought" she said "and trying to account for it. You know I missed all the childhood illnesses. I eat the right things. I've always been careful about that. And I take a lot of systematic exercises. I walk five to eight miles a day when I think I need it. Then I allow myself no negative thoughts. It's always what to do not what not to do. I avoid people who disconcert me. I simply won't be irritated. I also refrain from falling in love. I'm very careful about that. The love of my life is Mae West and I am conscientious about her welfare. Falling in love and worrying are against her welfare. She has to be pleased about colors and I see that she is. She has to have perfect temperatures and perfect order. Everything has to be arranged exactly as she likes it in this room, for example, even if all the furniture has to be moved. When I put on a show, it has to be my show completely. That's why I'm not in movies at present. I am offered script after script but they are not right for me. I think I shall possibly do a *Diamond Lil* again in color and widescreen but only if it is all mine.[67]

With her appearances and interviews, Mae West continued to define the term Diva, even though that term wasn't part of the

---

66 Hopper, Hedda. Mae West Chipper in Club Debut. Syndicated. July 19, 1954

67 Mae West Sweeps into Town in her Tour of the Club Circuit. *Buffalo News.* September 27, 1954.

lexicon just yet. But its traits were certainly being established by West, even if only unwittingly.

The censors continued to dog West and her work. When she was booked to bring her act to Chicago's Chez Paree in the winter of 1955, Tribune columnist Herb Lyon wrote:

> Have an inside tip. Good ol' Mae West, the c'mon-up-and-see-me gal, may hit a snag or three when she brings her dazzling new act to the Chez Paree Feb. 9. Mae cavorts with assorted Mr. Americas, and veteran night spotters who caught her in Vegas, Miami, and New York say the "material " is more sizzling than scintillating. Local police censors have been alerted and already have their ears up and their eyes open. Best guess is that La West will have to do some serious scissoring for the Chicago engagement.[68]

Sadly, about a week into her successful appearance in Chicago, Mae West's chauffeur committed suicide. A story in the Tribune stated:

> Authorities yesterday were investigating the apparent suicide of Ray Charles Wallace, 44, personal chauffeur for actress Mae West. His body was found Tuesday in Miss West's Cadillac limousine on a farm near Patoka, Ind. Miss West, currently appearing at a Chicago night club, said she could give no reason for Wallace's death. Her manager, Vincent Lopez, said Wallace left Miami on Feb. 7 to drive the car here. Lopez said Wallace called him several times en route to complain of having " lots of trouble." Lopez said he notified Indiana state police Sunday to be on the lookout for Wallace. Coroner Robert Kendall termed the death suicide. He said a hose ran from the exhaust pipe to the car's interior.[69]

---

68   Lyon, Ben. Tower Ticker. *Chicago Tribune.* January 27, 1955
69   Probe suicide of Chauffeur for Mae West. *Chicago Tribune.* February 17, 1955

Mae was still on tour doing her nightclub act in the spring of 1955 when she appeared at Ciro's in Los Angeles and her first leading man attended the show. Hedda Hopper stated in her column:

> Cary Grant fell in love with Mae West all over again when he showed up at her Ciro's opening, and the renewed romance may net them both a million bucks. Seeing Mae again gave Cary, who was her first leading man in films, the idea they should co-star in a remake of their first picture, *She Done Him Wrong*. It would be sensational and they'd not only make a fortune but history. No stars have repeated their original roles in a remake. You couldn't keep the customers away from that one with a machine gun. Cary went backstage to see Mae after the show, and says, "No woman in the world plays a part as well as Mae plays that character. She looks younger than when we worked together. Few people know that the secret of her vitality and youth is that she neither smokes nor drinks. Never has."[70]

No such film was made, or perhaps even seriously planned, but Hopper's column would frequently offer tantalizing possibilities to her readers.

At a June, 1956 engagement in Washington, there was an altercation among two of the muscle men who were part of Mae's act. According to a report in *The Los Angeles Times*:

> Mr. Universe, sporting a shiner and limping today, filed assault charges against a fellow muscle man who knocked him out last night in Mae West s dressing room. Mickey Hargitay filed charges against Chuck Krauser. Both are members of the Mae West troupe which is making a, nightclub appearance in Washington. Krauser pleaded self defense. His lawyers said they will seek a jury trial when the case comes up June 28. Miss West, garbed in a

---

70 Hopper, Hedda. Grant Would Co-Star Again With Mae West. Syndicated. May 16, 1955

pink duster over full black slacks, sat in silence throughout the hearing before the charges were filed. She kept silent even when another muscle man in the act, George Eiferman, suggested Krauser "planted a tremendous haymaker on Mickey s head" because he is in love with Miss West and was defending her against abusive language by Hargitay. Hargitay, 26, is a weight lifter with a build that won him, the Mr. Universe label in a competition at London last year. Municipal Court Attache Kenneth D. Wood took testimony from all present in Miss West's dressing room, including reporters who had been trying to conduct a news conference when the fists flew. Asked for her version, Miss West gestured toward Hargitay and replied: "He was standing at. the doorway and when he went like that" she threw up a diamond-laden hand "Chuck hit him."[71]

Krauser was a former wrestler. Hargitay was just in the process of divorcing his current wife so he could marry Jayne Mansfield, who was in the process of divorcing her current husband. They would remain married until Mansfield's tragic death in 1967, and were the parents of actress Mariska Hargitay. Krauser later changed his name to Paul Novak and became Mae's companion for the rest of her life.

The 1950s was the first golden age of television, with film and radio performers like Lucille Ball, Eve Arden, Abbott and Costello, Red Skelton, William Bendix, Jack Benny, Dennis O'Keefe Jackie Gleason, and others taking a crack at the small screen with various degrees of success. Rumors were abounding in 1956 that TV execs were considering Mae West for her own musical variety show. This prompted a reaction from columnist Jack Eigen which, when read today, offers an interesting window into the suppressive culture of the era where Elvis Presley had to be shown from the waist up:

____

71 Mae West's Muscle Men in Fist Fight. *The Los Angeles Times*. June 8, 1856

With horror we've been hearing that Mae West might be seen on TV in the near future. As far back as I can remember, and brother that's far, Mae has been known for exploiting sex on the stage. Everything she has ever said before an audience had a double meaning. She has to be blue to be seen. Now what on earth can she do on TV? People are complaining about horror programs; imagine what would happen with her on TV! She can't even walk without being suggestive. She would make Elvis Presley look like a choir boy.[72]

In 1957 the salacious magazine *Confidential* was in court with Mae West over an article she insisted was false, regarding herself and late prizefighter Chalky White, who was her chauffeur in the 1930s. Mae told the press: "Chalky was always a gentleman. They went to him and told him they were making a movie about my life. They promised him a small part in the picture. He later told me he didn't say any of the things they claim he did."[73]

In 1958, Mae West made a surprise appearance at the Academy Awards, doing a duet with Rock Hudson on the song "Baby It's Cold Outside." Cheered by the surprised crowd, this appearance resulted in more movie offers, and a younger fan base who had heard of her but had never seen her perform. An independent film company announced that Mae would return to movies in *Klondike Lou* with former leading men Cary Grant, George Raft, Randolph Scott, and Lloyd Nolan appearing in cameos. Producer Jerry Wald wanted to find a movie to star Mae West with Marilyn Monroe. Unfortunately, these projects never happened.

Mae West released her autobiography, *Goodness Had Nothing To Do With It* at the end of the 1950s, and went on a book tour to promote it. However, a TV appearance with Charles Collingwood on *Person to Person* was edited out of the show because of her typi-

---

72 Eigen, Jack. Jack Eigen Speaks. *Chicago Tribune.* August 4, 1956

73 Magazine Lied About Her and Boxer, Mae West Says. *The Los Angeles Times.* August 23, 1957

cally suggestive answers to his questions. Even in her 60s, Mae West was being censored. A review in the *Chicago Tribune* stated:

> This is a book about a gal in show business, but it contains precious little about show business as such. This is Mae West talking about Mae West humorously and light heartedly and with a philosophy as shallow as a pie pan. Included, along with memoirs of footlights and dressing rooms and prison cells and boudoirs and trysts in taxis, are her directions for the preservation of the feminine contours that caused American sailors in World War II to name a bulging life jacket after her. No other autobiography can make that claim.[74]

Mae's made another television appearance in 1959 on a special hosted by Dean Martin and also featuring Bob Hope. Delighted to be working with two men who understood comic timing, Mae traded quips with Hope and joined Dino for the duets "I Can't Give You Anything But Love" and "Personality," which also included a lot of comedy. The show was a hit.

In 1960, Red Skelton asked Mae to be a guest on his hit television series, telling her they could put together a skit that was funny and would also promote her book. She also was allowed the freedom of writing her own lines and approving the sketches in which she'd appeared. Satisfied, Mae agreed to make an appearance on Red's show. The sketch had Mae, as herself, being interviewed by an Edwin R. Murrow type, played by William Schallert. They do a brief interview where Mae responds with funny lines, and at one point says "be careful, the censor has a weak heart." She recalls old lovers she has and as she does skits with her responding to Red's characters like Cauliflower McPugg, Clem Kadiddlehopper, and San Fernando Red. Mae worked out the sketches with Skelton, adding her own lines, and the normally egotistical comedian stepped back and allowed Mae to get the lion's share of the

---

74 Leonard, William. Mae West, Author, Tells of Curves and Contours. *Chicago Tribune.* October 11, 1959

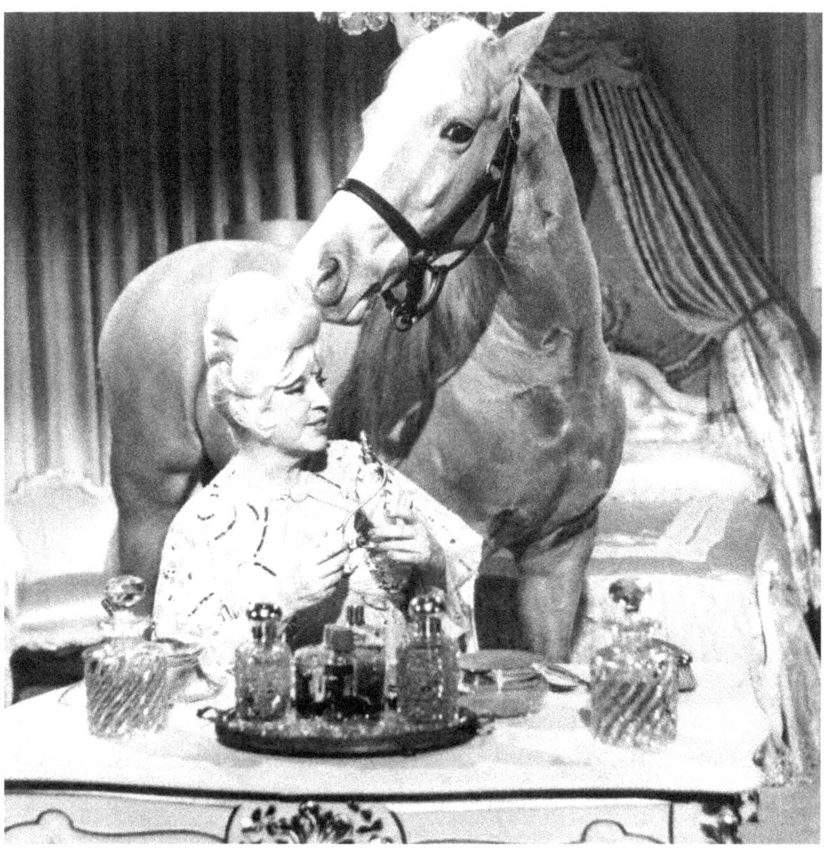

Mae West appeared in an episode of TV's Mister Ed

laughs. The show was a huge ratings success and her appearance also increased book sales.

In 1961, Mae West had a new play on stage entitled *Sextette*, about an older woman and her six husbands. A review of the show stated: "Through all the rapid action, Miss West has ample opportunity to show the humorous and tongue-in-cheek talk which has made her an internationally famous figure. She holds sway over her man as only Miss West can, and sports the most glamorous gowns of her fabulous career"[75] It would later be produced as a movie.

---

75   Mae West Currently Starring in Own Farce. *Suburbanite Economist.* July 6, 1961

The next time Mae appeared on TV was on a March 1964 episode of the popular show *Mister Ed* about a talking horse. While the Skelton show was live and on tape, *Mister Ed* was shot on film, making it West's first filmed appearance since *The Heat's On* 21 years earlier. While being seen on Skelton's variety show seemed appropriate enough, her appearance on a family program beloved by children seemed to be a bit daring for the times. However, there was another factor connected to this idea. The show's creator, Arthur Lubin, was interested in starring Mae in a series where she'd play a wisecracking private eye. Unfortunately, this was another idea that never materialized. Later that same year, Mae sued in court a lounge singer who was using the name Diamond Lil.

That same year, Mae was asked to co-star with Elvis Presley in the film *Roustabout*. Mae was intrigued, and interested in working with Elvis, but she didn't like the matronly role in the screenplay. Elvis contacted Mae, asking her to take the role, and she was charmed, but her demands were beyond what Presley's manager, Colonel Parker, would agree to. While the filmmakers were open to West writing her own dialog, Colonel Parker was hardly enthused with her insisting on billing above the title alongside Presley's name. Even when Mae agreed to allow Elvis's name to go first, only Presley was allowed billing above the title for his films. When she also requested a love scene with the singer, Mae West was told her services were no longer requested, and Barbara Stanwyck was hired for the role. It was to be Stanwyck's final theatrical film.

Movies continued to elude Mae West in the 1960s, despite many offers. Ross Hunter wanted her for *The Art of Love* (1965), but when she was not allowed to rewrite her role's dialog, she left the project and was replaced by Ethel Merman. Ferdrico Fellini wanted her to appear in his films *Juliet of the Spirits* (1965) and *Satyricon* (1969), but Mae didn't feel either part was suitable for her screen persona.

Mae was famously included on the cover of the Beatles' iconic LP *Sergeant Pepper's Lonely Heart's Club Band*. Many celebrities graced the cover montage of that record, and all signed releases allowing The Beatles to use their image, except for Bowery Boy Leo Gorcey, who wanted money. His image was removed. Mae initially refused, taking umbrage at the album's title, believing she would never be in a lonely heart's club. She finally agreed after each of the Beatles sent her a handwritten letter indicating their admiration and respect.

In 1969, the Academy of Motion Picture Arts and Sciences held a series of screenings celebrating Hollywood in the 1930s, with stars and filmmakers doing a Q&A after each. On the last night of the series, Mae West agreed to appear and take questions after a screening of *I'm No Angel*. The theater not only sold out, another 50 chairs were placed in the orchestra pit, and yet another 400-odd parties were turned away at the door. Mae West's popularity continued in the decades she made no movies. She had reached legendary status.

A 1970 feature on Mae in *Hollywood Studio Magazine* discussed her continued popularity now that her classic films were in circulation on TV and campus revival theaters:

> The grandma of all the super sex goddesses rolled into one, Mae reached the pinnacle of fame, fortune, and adoration more than 40 years ago, yet a visit to her shrine at the Ravenswood Apartments in Hollywood, or her palatial Santa Monica beach house is still a major happening. "I was never vulgar or obscene. I could act. I didn't need to take off all my clothes to keep the audience interested." A master of parody, the moralists of her heyday huffed and puffed about her goings on but the all missed the point. The point of Mae West's humor and parody was the fact she could move men to laughter not lust. While hardly sitting home counting her money, Mae has plenty of everything one could want in life. After 50 years of

being interviewed by reporters, Mae is the master of almost any situation.[76]

As the 1960s concluded, Mae West finally agreed to return to movies when she was offered the opportunity to play a role in a movie based on a controversial novel. The idea of having Mae West in the screen version of Gore Vidal's edgy sex exchange story *Myra Breckinridge* certainly made sense. It was a role that seemed so right for her and in a project that challenged the norm and pushed the envelope well past the edge, even during an era where movies were becoming bolder. Films that were rated for adults only were among the most impactful. In fact, the then-X-rated *Midnight Cowboy* would go on to win Best Picture at the Oscars, and while its rating was brought down to R later on, it remains one of the classic films released during the transition from 60s to 70s filmmaking. Many of her new fans on college campuses where excited about the controversial Vidal novel being released as a movie and featuring Mae West in her first screen role since *The Heat's On* in 1943. A lot had happened in movies since the war years, and during all of the various transitions in show business, Mae continued to thrive successfully. Unfortunately, *Myra Breckinridge* is one of the worst movies ever made.

76　Taylor, Frank. Hi Mae, Can I Still Come Up and See You? *Hollywood Studio Magazine.* July 1970

MYRA BRECKINRIDGE

Directed by Michael Sarne
Screenplay by Michael Sarne and David Giler based on the novel
by Gore Vidal
Produced by Robert Fryer, David Giler, James Cresson
Cinematography by Richard Moore
Film Editing by Danford B. Greene

Songs:
Secret Place
Music by John Phillips
Lyrics by John Phillips

Hard to Handle
Written by Otis Redding

You Gotta Taste All the Fruit
Music by Sammy Fain
Lyrics by Alan Bergman and Marilyn Bergman

Cast:
Mae West . . . . Leticia
John Huston . . . . Buck Loner
Raquel Welch . . . . Myra Breckinridge
Rex Reed . . . . Young Man
Farrah Fawcett . . . . Mary Ann
Roger C. Carmel . . . . Dr. Montag
Roger Herren . . . . Rusty
George Furth . . . . Charlie Flager, Jr.
Calvin Lockhart . . . . Irving Amadeus
Jim Backus . . . . Doctor
John Carradine . . . . Surgeon

Andy Devine . . . . Coyote Bill
Grady Sutton . . . . Kid Barlow
Robert P. Lieb . . . . Charlie Flager, Sr.
Skip Ward . . . . Chance
Kathleen Freeman . . . . Bobby Dean Loner
B.S. Pully . . . . Tex
Buck Kartalian . . . . Jeff
Monte Landis. . . . . Vince
Tom Selleck . . . . Stud
Michael Stearns . . . . Stud
Peter Ireland. . . . . Student
Nelson Sardelli . . . . Mario
William Hopper. . . . . Judge Frederic D. Cannon
Cal Bartlett. . . . . Letitia's Secretary
Russ McCubbin . . . . Leticia's Driver
Ron Nyman . . . . Chauffeur
Bill Chatham . . . . Chauffeur
Vic Christy. . . . . Spectator at Operation
Boyd Cabeen . . . . Spectator at Operation
Joe Pine . . . . Spectator at Operation
Don Ames . . . . Spectator at Operation
Ethelreda Leopold . . . . Bridge Party Guest
Judith Woodbury . . . . Bridge Party Guest
George Simmons . . . . Bridge Party Guest
Tony Regan . . . . Bridge Party Guest
Choo Choo Collins . . . . Party Guest
George DeNormand . . . . Party Guest
Duke Fishman . . . . Accident Witness
Richard LaMarr . . . . Accident Witness
Cosmo Sardo . . . . Accident Witness
Geneviève Waïte . . . . Dental Patient
James Gonzalez . . . . Patient
Michael Jeffers . . . . Patient
John Pedrini . . . . Patient
Ray Pourchot . . . . Patient

Chester Jones . . . . Waiter
Svetlana Mischoff. . . . . Student
Toni Basil. . . . . Cigarette Girl
Thordis Brandt. . . . . Whip-Cracking Masseuse
Luanne Roberts . . . . Painted Party Girl
Michael Sarne . . . . Acting School Student

Released June 24, 1970
Twentieth Century Fox
Running Time: 94 minutes

It is unfortunate that Mae West's first movie in over a quarter-century turned out to not only be her worst film, but one of the absolute worst movies ever made. *Myra Breckinridge* had been a controversial novel by Gore Vidal, written like a diary, and satirically exploring different levels of decadent sexuality while attacking the Hollywood system. When it was released in February of 1968, critics panned it as pornographic, resulting in it becoming a Best Seller. Twentieth Century Fox bought the films rights later that same year and filming began in 1969.

Vidal submitted a script, which was later rewritten by David Giler with Vidal's ultimate approval. The pre-production went through several changes until Michael Sarne was hired to direct. Sarne rewrote the screenplay to make it more jarring than Vidal's book had offered. Original director Bud Yorkin, for instance, was replaced because studio head Darryl Zanuck thought Yorkin's approach to the material would be too safe. The book was popular because of its controversial approach, and Zanuck felt Sarne had good ideas. The final draft of the script was the tenth version.

Raquel Welch, a new sex symbol in show business, was hired to play the title role. Mae West was sought to portray Letitia Van Allen, a casting agent who seduces potential young actors. Mae West recalled for columnist Kevin Thomas:

> George Cukor introduced me to Robert Fryer, the producer. He came up to my apartment to talk about doing

Myra Breckinridge was Mae's first movie in 27 years

Myra. I said first I want to do my own story *Sextette*, the one where I have six husbands. All my fans are waiting for me to do it, but as it turn out this one comes up now. I told him I'd read the script and said you don't want me to do Myra, but he said the other part was just as good. Of course, I've got to write it myself. Every time she opens her mouth, she's got to say something funny and sexy. My first line is "I'll be right with you, boys. Get your resumes ready." That was an innocent line when I thought of it. I kept repeating it then it dawned upon me. I never really had an agent, except this guy who was madly in love with me. I thought, gee, what's an agent do, so I asked Fred Apollo over at the William Morris office. My one experience with an agent was when I had this act in vaudeville with two boys *Mae West and the Girdard Bros* and they went to this agent that got us twice as much money. I thought that was pretty good. I used to go out in vaudeville between plays. Even then I'd write my own parts.[77]

Mae was "offered $350,000, top billing, a private dressing room decorated in white French provincial, and Edith Head as her costume designer. But what really sold West was Fryer's guarantee that she would have complete control over her dialog. She signed on and soon changed her character's name from Letitia to Leticia, contending that her friends mispronounce the name putting emphasis "on the tit."[78]

About co-star Raquel Welch, Mae told Thomas, "I saw her once on television. She's a pretty girl." And regarding the sexual content that goes beyond West's own double-entendre style, "Nudity is all right if it's done for art's sake. If it belongs in a picture, gives meaning to it, that's fine. But if they're just going to throw a naked body in to help the plot it's going to become monotonous."

Raquel Welch was hired for the title role after it had been turned down by Audrey Hepburn and Vanessa Redgrave. Mae West's role was offered first to Bette Davis, who thought Vidal's original book was disgusting, and Sarne wanted Mickey Rooney to play a role that ended up going to John Huston, best known for directing such classics as *The Maltese Falcon* and *The African Queen*. Lee Majors was offered the role of Rusty, turned it down, but suggested girlfriend Farrah Fawcett for Rusty's girlfriend. Film critic

---

77 Thomas, Kevin. Come Up To See Mae about Myra. *Los Angeles Times*. August 31, 1969

78 Watts, Jill. *Mae West: an Icon in Black and White* Oxford University Press. 2001

Mae West, Raquel Welch

and sometime actor Rex Reed took the role of Myron with the understanding that George Cukor would be directing and Davis and Rooney would be acting in the film. One of Leticia's men is newcomer Tom Selleck.

Despite being away from movies for decades, and not playing the title role, Mae West insisted on receiving top billing and she got it. It is unfortunate that *Myra Breckinridge* was, as critic and historian Leonard Maltin once wrote, "As bad as any movie ever made."

The plot of the film has a man named Myron Breckinridge (Rex Reed) seeking a sex change operation in Denmark. Once the operation takes place, he becomes Myra Breckinridge, a beautiful glamorous woman. Upon her return to America, Myra pursues an acting career, attending the theatrical school of her uncle Buck Loner (John Huston). Myra vividly dreams about classic Hollywood, interprets its intentions negatively, and comes up with a mission: "the destruction of the last vestigial traces of traditional manhood in the race in order to realign the sexes, thus reducing population while increasing human happiness and preparing for its next stage." She targets what she interprets as an ordinary couple – Rusty (Roger Herren) and Mary Ann (Farrah Fawcett), lures the man to her and attacks him anally with an artificial phallus. She then centers on Mary Ann, enticing her to experiment with her sexuality. In the meantime, Leticia van Allen (Mae West) continues her habit of seducing young men, eventually hooking up with Rusty. Meanwhile, Buck investigates Myra's claims and discovers there is no evidence of Myron having died. Admitting to the operation, Myra strips and reveals to Buck that no all of the male organ has been removed. The film ends with Myron waking up in the hospital, having been in a car accident. Mary Ann is the nurse, and there is a magazine on his bedside table with a cover story on Raquel Welch.

The production of *Myra Breckinridge* was fraught with disruption and the press reported on it pretty regularly. According to columnist Joyce Haber:

> Now to Fox and *Myra Breckinridge*, yet again (how can one stay away?), where the sabers are still drawn between director Michael Same and producer Robert Fryer, co-producer James Cresson and co-author David Giler. I'm told that director Same "requested" that neither Cresson nor Giler appear on the sound stage. "I haven't been down there for three weeks as it is," says Cresson, "so his request is rather gratuitous." Giler, on the other hand, was called for by star Mae West on Monday, and he obliged. One always obliges Miss West. For example, she has a clause in her contract that no other female can wear white or black in a scene with her. Raquel Welch, who plays Myra, had a black dress designed for their first scene together. Producer Fryer learned of this, and told Raquel she couldn't wear it. Raquel said, "Either I wear it or I don't play." Raquel appeared for work Friday morning and found that the dress in question had mysteriously disappeared from her

dressing room. Raquel went home and didn't return. But something must have been settled over the weekend, for the scene was shot Monday, with Mae wearing white and Raquel her (recovered) black gown.[79]

And when the film finally wrapped production after a tumultuous shooting, columnist Kevin Thomas offered this reaction:

> The storm tossed production of *Myra Breckinridge* ended three months behind schedule on Fox's Stage 6 as Mae West, in a razzle dazzle production number, not only scored a personal triumph hut affected a reconciliation between the film's always-at-odds producer and director. On a huge nightclub set, a mirrorized plastic dome literally held up by air, Miss West, in form-fitting black and ermine, turbanned and trimmed by Edith Head, last week slinked out from behind a fluted pillar onto a zebra-striped runway. The tremendous applause that greeted her spectacular star entrance came not only from the dress extras but the entire crew as well. Tearing into a torrid, hard rock rendition of an Otis Redding tune "Hard to Handle," Miss West was backed by a chorus of black male dancers in white-tie-and-tails. It was a magic, indeed unique, moment, created by Miss West's lifelong dedication to self-preservation and the expertise acquired from seven decades of entertaining. She was witty, she was daring and, above all, supremely dignified. It was entirely possible to believe that 27 years had not passed since Miss West's last picture. Only afterwards would you realize that it was also quite possible that in today's Hollywood the only movie cameras in town turning at that moment were on her, that by the next day the fabulous set of this unchanging lady would perhaps already be packed away in a box the size of a trunk. Miss West not only wrapped up *Myra Breckinridge* but also wrapped

---

79 Haber, Joyce. Back to Myra Breckinridge. *Los Angeles Times* October 23, 1969

her producer Robert Fryer and director Michael Same around her diamond-studded fingers. For when Sarne called "cut" for the last time Fryer found himself grabbing the long-haired, bearded young director and kissing him.

(It has been well-chronicled that during production they had not exactly been conducting a mutual admiration society.) "Hmm," purred Miss West, while being escorted back to her dressing trailer (a white-and-gold miniature of her Hollywood apartment). "Was it sexy enough?" she asked rhetorically. "Such panache. So direct, so cavalier," Sarne had said of Miss West earlier. "When she says a line like, 'Come up and see me sometime,' she's telling you a million stories about all the men who did come up to see her."[80]

When *Myra Breckinridge* was released in the summer of 1970, it was one of two movies that year to receive the fairly new MPAA rating of X, where moviegoers under 18 were not admitted. The other film, Russ Meyers' *Beyond the Valley of the Dolls* became something of a cult classic over time. *Myra Breckinridge* remains one of the worst movies ever to achieve a commercial release. The X rating had gotten some marginal respect as being more than just a rating for "dirty movies" when *Midnight Cowboy* won the Oscar while *Myra Breckinridge* was being filmed. However, once this film was released, the X rating returned to its previous stigma. The reviewer in *Time* magazine called it "an incoherent tale of sodomy, emasculation, autoeroticism and plain bad taste."[81] Vincent Canby in *The New York Times* panned the film and singled out Mae West, stating:

Miss West, now close to 80, has the figure of a cinched in penguin and a face made of pink-and-white plaster in which little holes have been left for her eyes and mouth. Indeed, when the camera came in for a close-up, I was

---

80 Thomas, Kevin. Mae Creates a Magic Moment. *Los Angeles Times.* March 28, 1970
81 Myra Breckinridge Review. *Time.* July 6, 1970.

reminded of the scene in *Catch-22,* the novel, when the soldiers in the hospital suspect that there is nobody inside the always silent, completely bandaged figure of the flyer lying on one of the ward beds. I'm not at all sure Mae West is really in *Myra Breckinridge.*[82]

There was further controversy regarding writer-director's Sarne's use of the Twentieth Century Fox film library and intersperse film clips of some of the studio's old classics. Clips from Laurel and Hardy movies are edited to make them look like a gay couple. The use of Shirley Temple in films from her years as a child actress was stopped by the government because Shirley Temple Black was then an Ambassador. Loretta Young sued to have any clips of her removed from the film, not wanting to be associated with such a production.

Gore Vidal denounced the film. Raquel Welch spent the rest of her life making fun of both the movie and her performance in it. But Mae West didn't care, she loved the attention she was getting this late in her life. And although a lot of her dialog was recycled from past movies and shows, it delighted audiences who were looking for exactly what Mae delivered. In fact, the greater freedoms allowed dialog like this:

> Mae: How tall are you?
>
> Man: I'm six feet and seven inches, ma'am
>
> Mae: Well, never mind the six feet, and let's talk about the seven inches.

Myra Breckinridge started off strong at the box office. Moviegoers were intrigued by a film version of a Best Selling "dirty book" and the cast was certainly enticing. However shortly after its opening, box office receipts fell sharply, due to word-of-mouth about how bad the movie was. It never made back its production costs.

---

82   Canby, Vincent. Myra Breckinridge Review. *The New York Times.* July 5, 1970

The film was re-released in 1978 with some edits, giving it an R rating. It was also released to home video with the final sequence in black and white to more clearly indicate the previous footage was a dream.

As with many bad movies from another time, *Myra Breckinridge* developed a fan following, essentially due to how bad it is. Those who approach the film in this manner found a way to enjoy it, which means the film's legacy does have some positive aspects.

MAE WEST IN THE 70S
Her Final Decade

Despite the debacle of *Myra Breckinridge* being a commercial flop and a critical disaster, Mae West's popularity increased as she entered the 1970s. This decade ushered in a new and interesting approach to filmmaking featuring young directors who had been inspired by the classic films of Hollywood as well as European releases of the 1930s and 1940s. Directors like Francis Ford Coppola and Martin Scorsese came into prominence in what was to be known as The New Hollywood. At the same time, classic movies became mainstream popular among younger people. Colleges were showing classic films on campus, and even high schools had special movie nights. Among the most popular vintage stars included Humphrey Bogart, The Marx Brothers, W.C. Fields, and Mae West. Groucho Marx and Mae West were still alive to take bows, and Mae enjoyed receiving fan mail from young people discovering her films.

Because of her renewed popularity among those not born when her best films were released, Mae West began appearing at college campus showings of her films, much to the delight of the students. A reporter for *Hollywood Studio Magazine* was on hand when Mae appeared at UCLA in 1971:

> Looking and acting like the greatest female impersonator of all time, she went to college and spoke to students who had just seen *I'm No Angel*, which she made before they were born. Undulating on stage, standing with her hand on her hip ("it's resting"), 77-year old Mae bridged the generation gap and showed the youngsters why their parents (and grandparents) regard her as a phenomenon. Students howled at such lines as "I used to be Snow

White but I drifted" and "It's not the men in my life, it's the life in my men that counts."[83]

However, to Mae's chagrin, W.C. Fields was the more popular classic film star, with several classic comedies in circulation, while Mae, having made less than ten movies during her heyday, was limited. Thus, her most frequently revived film was *My Little Chickadee* and most of the questions she was asked were about Fields. There were some who believed the two of them made several movies together. With Fields having died in 1946, Mae took the opportunity to downplay his contribution to *My Little Chickadee,* claiming she wrote the entire screenplay, while Fields' only contribution was the Chicago Molly bit during the barroom scene. She further claimed that Fields stubbornly insisted on a co-writing credit despite that marginal contribution. Of course, this is not true.

As the two living icons popular with young people in the 70s, a meeting between Mae West and Groucho Marx at Groucho's home was arranged in the summer of 1975. Steve Stoliar, Groucho's secretary, recalled this event in his book *Raised Eyebrows: My Years Inside Groucho's House*:

> Groucho and Mae West didn't really know each other well despite the fact that they'd both been working on Broadway in the twenties and at Paramount in the thirties. Although their paths crossed over the years, Groucho and Mae West tended to travel in different social circles. Although her mind seemed to be in top form, West required some assistance in walking across the room or even going down a few steps. Otherwise, for a woman in her 80s she was remarkably well preserved. Once she was comfortably situated on the couch, Groucho came down the hall and immediately greeted her with, "Hi'ya Mae! What do you hear from Bill Fields?" Mae immediately snapped back, "In your dreams, Groucho, in your dreams!" Her voice still had the sassy nasality that had become

---

83 One-Man Woman. *Hollywood Studio Magazine.* July, 1971

Groucho Marx and Mae West

her trademark. No sooner had Groucho finished asking about Fields than he launched into another sensitive query: "Didn't they throw you in the pokey once?" Mae smiled at Groucho's question and said, "Yeah, they did, but I always manage to wiggle out of tight situations like that," and wiggled her shoulders a little as she spoke. I just sat there watching these two dinosaurs converse. To me they were the king and queen of screen comedy in the thirties.[84]

The 1970s had just begun when Mae's status went beyond notoriety and was true popularity. As early as 1971, Suzy Knickerbocker stated in her popular syndicated column:

Although she has only made one film since *My Little Chickadee* 31 years ago (we'd all like to forget that horror *Myra Breckenridge*, wouldn't we?), Mae West is still the center of attraction when she goes to a Hollywood party. Maybe it's because she's larger than life and not afraid to be an outspoken old party when the spirit moves her. She's a cat among mice. Mae stole the show at Paul Newman and Joanne Woodward's thing for John Huston the other night. She had cloistered herself in the library. Then a whisper began to circulate among the lesser legends. "Mae West is in the library." Before you could try to say come up and see me some time they started lining up to say hello, breathlessly, to Mae baby. Take Barbra Streisand, for instance. She knelt at Mae's feet and cooed. "Oh, it's wonderful to see you! I've adored you always." Mae gave her a look and said, "Then stop imitating me." "Oh," cried Barbra, "I do it because I've always admired you. "Baby." said Mae from the depth of her bosom, "cut out the adoration. I invented the Mae West style and I want to keep it exclusively for myself." To Jules Stein, the multimillionaire head of MCA, Mae was a bit more cordial, even when he recalled, "Mae, I was playing the fiddle in the orchestra that backed you up in your vaudeville act on the Orpheum circuit. That was 1915, wasn't it?" Mae just nodded. She must be crazy about those fellows with long memories. Dinah Shore was next in line with a plea for Mae to come on her television show. Dinah never stops cooking. Next came Steve McQueen and Henry Fonda,

---

84 Stoliar, Steve. *Raised Eyebrows: My Years Inside Groucho's House*. General Publishing Group, 1996

who were terribly polite and all that, and after them came
Earl Blackwell, who could hardly say hello, so busy was
he writing down Mae's priceless ad libs. He plans to put
them in his Celebrity Register, which he's bringing out
next year. Tell it like it is, Earl.[85]

The 1970s was also the era of Women's Liberation, and because
Mae West was considered something of a pioneer regarding that
attitude, her reaction was sought by current journalists:

> Cultural forecasters are always predicting that a "new
> woman" broods like a storm cloud on the horizon. Will
> she finally appear among us dressed in olive-drab military
> fatigues, like a weather-woman, or will she wear mini-
> skirts and mod-tinted glasses like a radical chic Gloria
> Steinem? Several women I know are looking back to the
> frontier and finding that the "new woman" always existed
> in women pioneers and in such American folk heroines
> as Diamond Lil and Calamity Jane. I would add to their
> herstorical hall of fame a living emancipated lady who
> has always reminded us that sex can be funny and fun. I
> refer to Mae West, platinum blonde big mama of camp,
> who, at nearly 80, still wears satin strapless evening gowns
> and swirls of ostrich feathers, who still flashes double
> entendres as dazzling as the rhinestones on her fingers.
> At age 78, she appeared at a Hollywood press conference
> and smiled seductively at the assembled reporters, one
> of whom asked what she thought of women's liberation.
> "I'm all for it," she replied without a tremor in that sultry
> voice. "In what way are you for it?" someone shouted.
> Mae West, hand on hip, didn't hesitate. "All the way." A
> feminist screen writer in the crowd whispered, "Dig it,
> Mae West has always been a liberated woman. In her
> movies she was always calm, cool and in control. She
> could handle six-shooters and outfox snake oil salesmen.

---

85   Knickerbocker, Suzy. The Unconquered West. *New York Daily News.*
   October 8, 1971

And most important, she wrote her own lines." Some of her best literary lines appear in a 95-cent paperback titled *The Wit and Wisdom of Mae West*, which is fast becoming a racy little red book for young housewives, career women and movement militants. My own favorite liberated quotes include: "Gentlemen may prefer blondes, but who says blondes prefer gentlemen?" And, "Good women have no fun. The only good woman I can recall in history was Betsy Ross and all she ever made was a flag."[86]

It is probably no surprise that elderly Mae West's reaction to the New Hollywood and its dismantling of a lot of classic Hollywood conventions was not positive. But it was quite surprising that she spoke out against the new sexual freedoms in films. In an article announcing Mae's 80th birthday, she told columnist Bob Thomas: "I don't approve of it. It's just not right. I can see what's happening. The picture makers have run out of plots. Everything has been done on the screen already. Now they have no stories so they simply throw naked bodies at the audience. And showing the sex act! I think that's terrible. When I was making pictures. I couldn't even say 'hell' or 'damn' on the screen. The church people watched me like a hawk. Where are the church people today? How can they allow such things as you see on the screen?"[87]

Perhaps the most revealing interview Mae West gave in the 1970s was a Q&A with Larry Grobel of *Newsday* in 1975:

Q: You once said that if you had ever depended on what other people were going to do with you, there could never have been a Mae West.

A: That's right. They didn't know what to do. I knew myself what I wanted and what to do.

Q: Which was?

---

86   Reinholz, Mary. Go West, Women. *New Yor News Magazine*. May 21, 1972
87   Thomas, Bob. Mae West Turns 80. Syndicated. August 20, 1973

A: Just what I've done. I'm really two people. I had to write all my plays and screenplays. I told Paramount to write material for me, just let me be the star, but Adolph Zukor (then head of Paramount) said I knew what the public wanted better than he did.

Q: Has there ever been a time when you wanted to break out of the Mae West mold?

A: What could I be? I've never been anything else. Everyone wants to be Mae West, why shouldn't I?

Q: How did you develop your sense of timing?

A : I got that from songs I sung with punchlines and rhythm, when I was a child. I talked with rhythm. I don't know about other people. I've been so absorbed in myself since I've been a child. I've never been interested in anybody but myself. Just me, me. What other woman in the world has done what I've done? I've never done anything that wasn't a success

Q: Which of the roles that yon have played have you enjoyed most?

A: All of them.I never did anything I didn't like. I had the say over most of my pictures because I wrote most of my stories.

Q: What about *Myra Breckinridge*?

A: There was no story in it. I wrote one in there but they took it out.

Q: What did you think of Raquel Welch, who acted in the picture with you?

A: She did all right. She'd be what we'd call a "meany" a woman second lead who was a mean character. But they put her in lead parts and she's really second lead.

Q: What about Marilyn Monroe? A: I never saw her much. The William Morris office thought they had another Mae West when they got her. But her sex was schoolgirl sex.

Q: Who are some of your favorite actors and actresses?

A: Cary Grant I liked him so well I had him twice in *She Done Him Wrong* and *I'm No Angel*. I liked James Cagney and Humphrey Bogart. And Paul Muni. One of the greatest new personalities is George Segal.

Q: What about W. C. Fields?

A: He was all right.

Q: Do you really mean that?

 A : He was envious of me. Everyone told him *My Little Chickadee* was his best thing.

Q: I'd like to get your opinion of the women's movement

A: I think it's a good thing. I'm for it. I always went ahead and did what I wanted to do. What I always resented was a man could have an affair with anyone he wanted but a woman wasn't supposed to. I rebelled against that.

Q : In 1969 Life magazine did a cover story on you. "At 75, Mae West is a masterpiece of self-preservation," they wrote. You still are. How have you done it?

A: Mental and physical activity. I have an Exercycle in my kitchen, a walking machine, weights. I do calisthenics. When I'm at my house on the beach I walk on the sand. My thinking's the same as it's always been. I feel the same. My weight's stayed within five pounds of what it's always been. I look the same. Never had any plastic surgery. I have beautiful hands, people are always telling me about my hands. My teeth are all mine. My measurements are the same.

Q: You've said that your life has been a prelude to what you still hope to do. Can we end with the future tense?

A: I'm gonna do more and more and more. I'm so busy. There are albums being planned, shows, songs. There's talk of a TV show. I just go on and on and on.[88]

Mae West did appear to indeed "go on and on." In the bicentennial year of 1976, it was announced that Mae West was once again returning to movies. Arrangements were made for Mae to make a motion picture version of her 1961 play *Sextette* about an older woman marrying a much younger man who discovers he is actually her sixth husband. Plans were made to include star cameos as the various husbands and, even though she was 15 years older than she had been in the play, and was playing an older woman then, it was still believed she could pull off the role effectively. Unfortunately, while *Sextette* was not as bad a movie as *Myra Breckinridge*, it certainly wasn't a good enough film to be Mae West's movie swan song.

---

88   Grobel, Larry. An Immodest Mae West. *Newsday* February 9, 1975

SEXTETTE

Directed by Ken Hughes
Screenplay by Herbert Baker from the play by Mae West
Produced by Daniel Briggs, Robert Sullivan
Cinematography by James Crabe
Film Editing by Argyle Nelson

Songs:
Love Will Keep Us Together
Neil Sedaka - Howard Greenfield

Next Next
Composed and conducted by Van McCoy
Performed by Alice Cooper

After You've Gone
Written by Henry Creamer and Turner Layton

Happy Birthday Twenty One
Written by Neil Sedaka and Howard Greenfield

Honey Pie
Written by John Lennon and Paul McCartney

Cast:
Mae West . . . . Marlo Manners
Timothy Dalton . . . . Sir Michael Barrington
Dom DeLuise . . . . Dan Turner
Tony Curtis . . . . Alexei Andrea Karansky
Ringo Starr . . . . Laslo Karolny
George Hamilton . . . . Vance Norton
Alice Cooper . . . . Singing Waiter

Keith Allison . . . . Waiter in Alexei's Suite
Rona Barrett. . . . . .Rona Barrett
Van McCoy . . . . .Delegate
Keith Moon . . . . .Dress Designer
Regis Philbin . . . . .Regis Philbin
Walter Pidgeon . . . . .The Chairman
George Raft . . . . .George Raft
Gil Stratton . . . . .Gil Stratton
Harry Weiss . . . . .The Godfather
Rick Leonard . . . . .Team Mascot
June Fairchild. . . . . .Woman Reporter
George E. Carey. . . . . .Dockweiler
Ed Beheler . . . . .President Jimmy Carter
Peter McWilliams . . . . .Ronald Cartwright
Sasha Hoyningen-Huene. . . . . . . .Kellner
Derek Murcott. . . . . .Hotel Manager
William Beckley. . . . . .Desk Clerk
Ed Ness . . . . .1st Deaf and Dumb Man
Jay B. Larson . . . . .2nd Deaf and Dumb Man
Richard Peel. . . . . .English Chef Christopher
Ian Abercrombie . . . . .BBC announcer Rex
. . . . .Ambrose
John Austin . . . . .Reporter
James Bacon. . . . . .Reporter
Peter Liapis . . . . .Ronald Cartwright
Jill Freeman . . . . .Fan
Jason Cooper . . . . .Guard
Cal Bartlett. . . . . .Mr. Foreman
Brent Williams. . . . . .All American Gymnast
. . . . .Trampolinist
Brian Abadie . . . . .Weight-lifter Mr. California Jr.
Ric Drasin . . . . .Weight-lifter Mr. California
Denny Gable . . . . .Shot Putter Mr. U.S.A.
Reg Lewis . . . . .Athlete
Jim Morris . . . . .Weight-lifter Mr. America

Kal Szkalak. . . . . .Athlete Mr. America
Jim Tarleton . . . . .Weight-lifter Mr. Pennsylvania
Mike Besikof . . . . .Weight-lifter
Dave Du Pre . . . . Weight-lifter
Roger Callard. . . . . Javelin Thrower
Joel Goodman . . . . The marathon runner
Ben Astar . . . . Israeli Delegate
Patrick Sullivan Burke . . . . Irish Delegate
Nassir Cortbawi . . . . Lebanese delegate
Rollin Moriyama . . . . Japanese Delegate
Hansu Mehta. . . . . East Indian delegate
Harold Fong. . . . . Chinese Kitchen Chef
Jorge Moreno . . . . Spanish Kitchen Chef
Klair Bybee. . . . . Karolny's Cinematographer
Bob Harks . . . . Official
John Hugh McKnight . . . . Gambler
Gene Montoya. . . . . Dancer
Don Banashek . . . . Bodyguard
Alan Cope . . . . Man waving bowler hat
Bonnie L. DeSouza . . . . Fan

Released March 3, 1978
Crown International Pictures
Running Time: 91 minutes

Sextette was such a fiasco its backstory is far more interesting than the film itself. However, unlike *Myra Breckinridge*, it retains somewhat of a campy quality with cameos by the likes of Keith Moon, Ringo Starr, Alice Cooper, George Hamilton, Tony Curtis, and even old friends George Raft and Walter Pidgeon.

The idea for Mae to do more movies came about after she was signed to appear in *Myra Breckinridge*. Producers contacted Mae with the idea of turning her Broadway shows into films now that censorship restrictions were more open. In subsequent interviews, Mae would loftily claim that many of her shows were set to become movies with her screenplays and her starring. But it wasn't until the Spring of 1976 when the idea of *Sextette* was announced:

> "Mae Day" is not a cry of distress nor a celebration of the workers arising, but a tribute to durable actress Mae West, who is going before the cameras again at 83. Mayor Tom Bradley proclaimed May 1 "Mae Day" in honor of Miss West and will present a scroll to her at a dinner Friday acclaiming her "valuable and important role" in the movie industry. Miss West is scheduled to begin work July 1 in her first starring role since *The Heat's On* in 1943. filming *Sextette* based on *Sex*. the Broadway play she wrote that made her a star in 1926.

Actually, *Sextette* was based on a play Mae performed on stage in 1961 with Jack LaRue and Alan Marshall as her leading men. The play opened in Chicago, and during its run Marshall died of a heart attack on stage in July of that year.

This resulted in a spate of interviews printed in the newspapers for the remainder of the year, reminding everyone of Mae West's natural wit, and delighting those who had discovered her classic pre-code films on television. Mae was forthcoming about her age without reservation, and believed she could still pull off the role of a sexy woman despite being in her 80s. The audition for her leading man resulted in hundreds of applicants, but she settled on British actor, and future James Bond, Timothy Dalton.

Originally set for a $4 million budget with Mae receiving $1 million, that changed to a $2.5 million budget with Mae receiving $250,000 and 20% of the profits after it was difficult to find backers. Herbert Baker was hired to write the screenplay based on Mae West's play. Having written several films for Dean Martin and Jerry Lewis, Baker knew comedy well. However, A.J. Palermo wrote a Letter to the Editor in *The Los Angeles Times*, claiming he wrote the original screenplay that got the movie approved and never received screen credit. Irving Rapper was set to direct. Rapper had directed Bette Davis in several films, including the classic *Now Voyager* (1942). However, by the time of *Sextette*, he was getting on

Ad for Sextette

in years, and reportedly came on the set and asked, "where's Bette?" Rapper (who lived many more years, dying a month before is 102nd birthday), was eventually replaced by Ken Hughes, who had co-written and directed *Chitty Chitty Bang Bang* (1968).

When production began in December of 1976, Mae needed to be helped around the set and had an earpiece where director Hughes would feed her lines. Her deliver was still good and she came alive during the song numbers, including a cheeky rewording of Neil Sedaka's "Happy Birthday Sweet 16" to "Happy Birthday 21." The producers wanted to capitalize on Mae's popularity with high school and college students, so they dotted the cast with cameos from the likes of Ringo Starr, Alice Cooper, and drummer for The Who, Keith Moon. Moon especially has fun camping up his small role. From the other perspective, Mae insisted on small parts for the aforementioned Walter Pidgeon and George Raft. It was sentimentally fitting that Raft appear in Mae's last movie, having starred in her first. She also wanted Cary Grant, but he retired from the screen after *Walk Don't Run* (1967) and refused.

Mae West plays Marlo Manners, about to go on a honeymoon with her sixth husband Sir Michael Barrington (Timothy Dalton). They head to a honeymoon suite at a high class London hotel, arranged by her manager Dan Turner (Dom DeLuise). Meanwhile, an international conference is taking place at the same hotel, with the delegates disruptively trying to get a look at Marlo while the chairman (Walter Pidgeon) tries to maintain order. Consummation of the marriage is constantly interrupted by interviews, photo sessions, and the appearance of men wanting to be alone and attempt to seduce Marlo, including athletes and former husbands.

One ex, Alexei (Tony Curtis) is a Russian delegate at the conference, and insists on one last fling with Marlo before he will proceed with negotiations.

There are a series of various comic situations, such as Barrington calling himself "gay" in an interview with Rona Barrett, not realizing his word for happy also was slang for homosexual, and Marlo

George Raft was in Mae's first film, and her last

dealing with husbands being played by Tony Curtis, George Hamilton, and Ringo Starr, each camping it up with abandon. While Mae singing is fun and remarkably well paced, the film could have done without Dom DeLuise camping it up doing Paul McCartney's Beatle song "Honey Pie," or Timothy Dalton singing Neil Sedaka's "Love Will Keep Us Together," which had been a huge hit for The Captain and Tenille the year before. Notably, the lyric "someday your looks will be gone," is changed to "your looks will never be gone."

Due to a series of setbacks, the budget ballooned very quickly and by the time production ended, nearly $7 had been spent. The producers became desperate to get the movie released and get some of their costs back and hastily put together a couple of screenings. Premieres were held in 1977, one for just the cast and crew, and another open to the public. The latter, which took place at the Bruin Theater, was filled with Mae West's new young fans who gave her a standing ovation. Mae was quite moved by their response. However, these premieres worked against the film. Word got out to the studios that *Sextette* was terrible and they all backed away from releasing it. The producers then planned to distribute the movie themselves. Eventually it was picked up by Crown International for release in 1978, but its bookings were scant and it only grossed $50,000, a colossal failure.

The critics who bothered to review *Sextette* had nothing redeeming to say about it. Vincent Canby of *The New York Times* stated:

> *Sextette* is a disorienting freak show in which Mae West, now 87 years old, does a frail imitation of the personality that wasn't all that interesting 45 years ago. The movie is a poetic, terrifying reminder of how a virtually disembodied ego can survive total physical decay and loss of common sense. The character we see in this peculiar film looks less like the Mae West one remembers from even *Myra Breckinridge* than like a plump sheep that's been stood on its hind legs, dressed in a drag-queen's idea of chic, bewigged and then smeared with pink plaster. The creature inside this getup seems game but arthritic and perplexed. She walks with apparent difficulty. One eye sometimes sags and the voice, despite Hollywood's electronic skills, cracks like the voice of the old lady she really is. Under these circumstances, the sexual innuendos are embarrassing. Granny should have her mouth washed out with soap, along with her teeth. The movie was directed by Ken Hughes, a fellow you might think had better things to do than to prop up the Tower of Pisa. The real problem with *Sextette* is neither the passage of time nor the erosion of talent. There was never a great deal of talent there to begin with. Miss West's function in the early 30's was to send up and get around the hypocritical moral prohibitions of the day. It made her famous but then the times passed her by. *My Little Chickadee* is the only film she ever

made that's still worth seeing today, but its star is W.C. Fields, not Miss West who, in the presence of a comedian of Fields's great character, comes across as monotonous and mean-spirited....[89]

Canby's review is mean-spirited and inaccurate (*My Little Chickadee* is not the only Mae West movie that holds up), but it is a good indication of how contemporary critics responded to West's continuing to present the same image while up in her 80s (she was 84, not 87, at the time of Canby's review).

Many thought *Sextette* was cruel; an attempt by producers to exploit an elderly woman who falsely believed she was still the sexy image she had created as a young woman. Others were chagrined that elderly comedian George Burns could show up at events with a young escort on each arm and was applauded as an old rascal, while Mae West looked creepy working with much younger muscle men. In any case, *Sextette* was a bad movie and, now that it is older than *She Done Him Wrong* was when it was released, this travesty has been blissfully forgotten and Mae's classic films of the 1930s have lived on.

---

89 Canby, Vincent. Sextette review. *The New York Times*. June 8, 1979

THE FINAL YEAR

Despite the failure of *Sextette,* Mae West's admirers were still great in number. She planned to do a movie version of *Catherine Was Great* but, much to her spirit's chagrin, Mae was starting to slow down. In the late summer of 1979, West agreed to do a series of commercials for Poland Spring bottled water. Her voice and manner still registered as roughly the same, so without the visual of a much older woman, it sounded like Diamond Lil doing the ads with lines like "I invited the boys from Poland Spring to come up and see me sometime."

As she entered the 1980s, Mae West became more infirm. She would have good days, like when she attended a party and sang "Frankie and Johnny" to the delighted partygoers, and bad days when she seemed confused and incoherent. Mae was turning 87 in August of 1980 and planned on big party to celebrate, but suffered a stroke a week before her birthday. She fell out of bed, and when Novak went to her, she was unable to talk, and then started to cry. Novak told the press that she fell out of bed while dreaming about Burt Reynolds, which was the type of thing Mae would tell her fans.

In September of 1980, Mae suffered another stroke. She initially showed signs of some improvement but despite the efforts of everything from medical specialists to faith healers, it became evident to all that Mae West was dying. Her fancy bedroom was now equipped with a hospital bed and Novak hired an around-the-clock medical staff.

Mae West died on November 22, 1980. She was eulogized in newspapers and on TV news shows throughout the world. It was the end of a true icon of entertainment who never really stopped working. *The San Francisco Examiner* stated:

> Legendary Hollywood bombshell Mae West who starred
> in vaudeville, plays and films as a brassy, bosomy sex

Mae West died in November of 1980

symbol of the 1920s and '30s died yesterday at her apartment at the age of 87. "At 1030 she just closed her eyes.
Thank God it was peaceful and there was no pain," said
Jerry Martin, of the William Morris Agency, Miss West's
longtime public relations representative. "She'd been
home almost a month and she was doing fine," Martin
said yesterday. "She was so glad to be home. But this
morning when she got up she was having trouble breath-
ing." Martin said that Paul Novak, a former muscleman
in Miss West's nightclub act and her companion of the
last 25 years, called the doctor who examined the actress
and said that nothing further could be done. Novak was

with her at her death, Martin said. Last rites were performed by a priest who was summoned from a nearby church, Martin said. The aging sex queen died just three weeks after leaving a hospital where she had spent three months recuperating from a mild stroke that left her speech impaired. Miss West remained amazingly attractive far into her twilight years. In an interview when she was 83, her figure still had that famous hourglass look. She attributed her good condition to the fact that she exercised, watched her diet, drank only a little champagne, didn't smoke, and was possessed of a third and extra thyroid gland. "Sex is like a small business," she said. "You gotta watch over it"[90]

Two days later, Mae's friend and co-star George Raft died of the emphysema he had been suffering from for some time. Raft had been instrumental in getting Mae West into movies, thus expanding her audience. It was somewhat poetic that these two screen icons should go together.

Mae West is one of the truly remarkable entertainers in 20th century show business. Performing almost through that entire century, she explored beyond the parameters of what was generally considered acceptable and challenged the norm in every level of entertainment. This book has concentrated on her motion picture work, because that is her lasting legacy by which she is represented. We benefit greatly from her agreeing to play the role in *Night After Night* when George Raft recommended her. And we benefit from her strength of character, insisting on writing her own screenplays and supervising her films. The image she created and cultivated lasted her throughout her life, and lives on in films like *She Done Him Wrong* and *I'm No Angel*. She paved the way for later women to write, direct, and star in their own films; supervising productions to create a lasting image. Mae West is one of the most important figures in entertainment history.

---

90   Sex Symbol Mae West Dies. *San Francisco Examiner.* November 23, 1980

BIBLIOGRAPHY

BOOKS

Chandler, Charlotte. *She Always Knew How.* NY: Simon and Schuster. 2009

Eyman, Scott. *Cary Grant: A Brilliant Disguise.* NY: Simon and Schuster. 2020

Leonard, Maurice. *Mae West Empress of Sex.* NY: Harper Collins, 1991

Louvish, Simon. *Mae West: It Ain't No Sin.* Thomas Dunne Books. 2005

McCann, Graham. *Cary Grant, A Class Apart.* NY: Columbia University Press, 1996

Neibaur, James L. *The W.C. Fields Films.* Jefferson, NC: McFarland 2017.

Neibaur, James L. *The George Raft Films.* BearManor Media. 2022

Stoliar, Steve. *Raised Eyebrows: My Years Inside Groucho's House.* General Publishing Group, 1996

Tucker, David C. *Rochelle Hudson: A Biography and Career Record.* Jefferson, NC: McFarland, 2023

Watts, Jill. *Mae West: an Icon in Black and White* Oxford University Press. 2001

West, Mae. *Goodness Had Nothing To Do With It.* Avon. 1959

Zukor, Adolph and Dale Kramer. *The Public is Never Wrong.* NY: Putnam, 1953

ARTICLES and REVIEWS

Bacon, James. More Women Than Men Come to See Mae. Syndicated. Associated Press. December 6, 1954

Bob Thomas syndicated column. Associated Press February 17 1947

Canby, Vincent. Sextette review. *The New York Times.* June 8, 1979

Chapman, John. Diamond Lil review. *The New York Daily News.* February 7, 1949

Chapman, John. Mae West Gives History The 0-0 In Lavish Catherine Was Great. *New York Daily News.*August 4, 1944

Corbett, Mae West, Many More at Proctor's. *Newark Star-Eagle.* September 23, 1913.

Cunningham, James. Asides and Interludes. *Motion Picture Herald.* July 30, 1932

Daly, Phil M. Along The Rialto. The Film Daily. March 12, 1936

Daniel, Frank. Diamond Lil Held Over She Done Him Wrong: Banned in Atlanta Continues Its Engagement After 'Capacity Week at the Buckhead Theater. *Atlanta Constitution.* April 16, 1933

Eigen, Jack. Jack Eigen Speaks. *Chicago Tribune.* August 4, 1956

Erskine Johnson column. Syndicated. November 5, 1942

Every Day's a Holiday review. *Picture Play.* October, 1938

Exhibitor Answers Hearst Attack. *Motion Picture Herald.* March 7, 1936

Goin to Town review. *Film Daily.* April 25, 1935

Grobel, Larry. An Immodest Mae West. *Newsday* February 9, 1975

Haber, Joyce. Back to Myra Breckinridge. *Los Angeles Times* October 23, 1969

Hartwell, Susan. The New Streamlined Mae West. *Silver Screen.* May, 1935

Hearst Papers Steam Up on West Pic So Far a Boon to the B.O. *Variety.* March , 1936

Hedda Hopper's Hollywood. *The Los Angeles Times*. November 16, 1939

Hopper, Hedda. Grant Would Co-Star Again With Mae West. Syndicated. May 16, 1955

Keats, Patricia. Sex is Beautiful. *Silver Screen*. November, 1933

Hopper, Hedda. Mae West Chipper in Club Debut. Syndicated. July 19, 1954

Klondike Annie Review. *The New York Times*. March 12, 1936

Knickerbocker, Suzy. The Unconquered West. *New York Daily News*. October 8, 1971

League of Decency Planned For Radio. *Evening Vanguard*. December 15, 1937

Leonard, William. Mae West, Author, Tells of Curves and Contours. *Chicago Tribune*. October 11, 1959

Lorenz, Alice. Mae West Soft on the Eyes. *Picture Play*. August, 1933

Lyon, Ben. Tower Ticker. *Chicago Tribune*. January 27, 1955

Mae West is Back Again. *Los Angeles Daily News*. July 8, 1943

Mae West Currently Starring in Own Farce. *Suburbanite Economist*. July 6, 1961

Mae West Due Nov. 4. *Democrat and Chronicle* Rochester, NY. October 20, 1946

Mae West Gives Film Capital Exhibitions as Smasher of Traditions. *Oakland Tribune*. December 11, 1932

Mae West Situation. *Independent Exhibitors Film Bulletin*. January, 1938

Mae West Sweeps into Town in her Tour of the Club Circuit. *Buffalo News*. September 27, 1954.

Mae West Tells How to Get a Man. *Screenland* December 1933

Mae West – Very Clever Woman. *The Bangor Daily*. December 17, 1912

Mae West's Methods Won't Land Husband, Says Reader. *The Spokane Press*. November 2, 1933

Mae West's Muscle Men in Fist Fight. *The Los Angeles Times*. June 8, 1856

Magazine Lied About Her and Boxer, Mae West Says. *The Los Angeles Times*. August 23, 1957

May West guest of Mae West at Chinese Theater. *Los Angeles Daily News*. October 25, 1933

New Acts This Week. *Variety*. July, 11, 1916

Night After Night review. *The New York Daily News*. October 29, 1932

Night After Night review. *Time Out*. September 10, 2012

Night After Night review. *Laura's Miscellaneous Musings*. June 22, 2021

No Signature. *Post-Crescent*. April 22, 1935.

Olson Bandies Letters with Mae West. *The Sacramento Union*. January 22, 1941

One-Man Woman. *Hollywood Studio Magazine*. July, 1971

Probe suicide of Chauffeur for Mae West. Chicago Tribune. February 17, 1955

Read Placards Town with Goin' To Town Cards. *Motion Picture Herald.* July 20, 1935

Reinholz, Mary. Go West, Women. *New Yor News Magazine.* May 21, 1972

Riley, Thomas Nord. Battle of the Sexes. *Hollywood.* 1940

Row Stirred By Radio Skit. *Los Angeles Times.* December 17, 1937

Schallert, Elza. Go West If You're an Adult. *Motion Picture.* May, 1933

Scheuer, Phillip K. She Done Him Wrong review. *The Los Angeles Times.* January 31, 1933

Sennwald, Andre. Belle of the Nineties review. *The New York Times.* September 22, 1934

Sex Symbol Mae West Dies. *San Francisco Examiner.* November 23, 1980

Shapiro, Vic. I'm No Angel Review. *Motion Picture Daily.* October 5, 1933

Stengel, Fred. The Heat's On review. *Motion Picture Daily.* November 29, 1943

Stop Lewd Films. *San Francisco Examiner.* February 29, 1936

Taylor, Frank. Hi Mae, Can I Still Come Up and See You? *Hollywood Studio Magazine.* July 1

Tenant, Madge. Mae West, Broadway's Most Daring Actress, Drops Into Hollywood. *Movie Classic.* September, 1932.

The Heat's On review. *Film Daily.* December 3, 1943

Thirer, Irene. She Done Him Wrong review. *The New York Daily News.* February 10, 1933

Thomas, Bob. Mae West Turns 80. Syndicated. August 20, 1973

Thomas, Kevin. Come Up To See Mae about Myra. *Los Angeles Times.* August 31, 1969

Thomas, Kevin. Mae Creates a Magic Moment. *Los Angeles Times.* March 28, 1970

Two Men Seized For Robbery of Mae West, Actress, in Los Angeles. AP Syndicated story. December 5, 1933

What the Picture Did For Me. *Motion Pictured Herald.* November 18, 1933

What The Picture Did For Me. *Motion Picture Herald.* November-December, 1934

What the Picture Did for Me. *Motion Picture Herald.* October 5, 1935

What The Picture Did For Me. *Motion Picture Herald.* April 16, 1938

INDEX